THE EFFECTIVE ADHD PARENTING GUIDE

15 EASY-TO-IMPLEMENT STRATEGIES TO IMPROVE
COMMUNICATION, COPE WITH OUTBURSTS, REDUCE
STRESS, AND SUPPORT ACADEMIC AND SOCIAL
SUCCESS

T. NICOLE

NONFICTION
NUCLEUS

TABLE OF CONTENTS

INTRODUCTION

Daniel's having a meltdown, and this time, it's right smack in the middle of the cereal aisle. He's grabbing stuff off the shelves, knocking over displays, and screaming at the top of his lungs.

His mom? She's seen it all before. Her face is as red as a tomato, and she can feel everyone's eyes on them. Talk about embarrassing. She can practically hear their thoughts, and it only makes her feel worse.

Trying to keep her cool, Tara tries to talk some sense into Daniel, but that just winds him up even more. Her heart's pounding, and she's trying to get a handle on the situation. But with all the noise and chaos, she's finding it hard to think straight.

At that moment, Tara feels stuck, unsure, and doesn't know what to do. She wishes there was a magic wand or something to help her son, to make others see that his tantrums don't reflect her parenting skills. But in that grocery store, under the weight of everyone's stares, all she can do is hold back the waterworks and do her best to calm Daniel down.

WHEN YOUR CHILD HAS ADHD

Having a kid with ADHD isn't a piece of cake. It's not just about handling the obvious stuff, like hyperactivity and impulsivity; there's a whole other side to it that only people in the same boat can understand.

From the endless worrying about their kid's grades to the toll it takes on their own mental and emotional health, having a kid with ADHD means extra stress, worry, and daily battles you can't see. In moments like grocery store tantrums, parents face judgment ("That kid's got no respect.") and unwanted advice ("Too much sugar!"). But what these people don't see is the hours spent looking up treatments, fighting for their kid's needs, and making sure their home is a safe and nurturing place. It's a constant juggling act, and sometimes, it's just too much.

About six million kids aged 3–17 years have been diagnosed with ADHD, showing just how common it is (Centers for Disease Control and Prevention, 2022). One of the biggest hurdles is dealing with behavioral issues. Kids with ADHD often struggle with impulsivity, hyperactivity, and keeping their attention focused. These behaviors can lead to conflicts at home, at school, and when hanging out with friends.

Kids with ADHD might find it hard to express themselves clearly or understand social cues. This means things can get very complicated when it comes to talking to their parents. More often than not, things end in frustration and misunderstanding. Then there's school and social situations. They might find it hard to make and keep friends because they're impulsive and have trouble controlling their emotions. At school, they might find it difficult to stay focused, finish tasks, and keep up with their classmates.

All this stress starts to add up for parents. You love your child and want the best for them, but dealing with their symptoms and how society sees them can really mess with your mental and emotional health. Worrying about your kid's future is overwhelming, stressful, and honestly, pretty lonely. But you're not alone.

Making It Work With an ADHD Child

Whether you're a parent or caregiver, single or married, you want some guidance on how to handle the challenges of raising a kid with ADHD. You're eager to understand their symptoms and how to support their behavior, and you're looking for practical advice and strategies for handling communication difficulties, tantrums, and stress. And let's not forget about school. As much as anyone, I understand how important it is to help them succeed in school and socially. Supporting their well-being, improving their relationships, and helping them thrive in all areas of life is a goal we all share, right?

Well, you're in for a treat with *The Effective ADHD Parenting Guide.* Imagine your home is like a lab, and you're the wise scientist mixing the right elements to create harmony. You apply these ADHD strategies, and communication with your kid just flows. You're talking, they're talking, and it's actually working. Tantrums? You've got the magic touch now; stress levels dip, and that calm you craved becomes your new normal. Think, too, about your child's confidence blooming right before your eyes. They're making friends, acing tasks, getting the hang of socializing. School's not a battlefield anymore, and homework's done without the threat of World War III.

And you, you're at the heart of this transformation. You're the one in charge of these tools, shaping a world where your child doesn't just get by but lives happily. With every strategy, you're chipping away at the pain, replacing it with progress and pride.

This isn't just theory; it's real change, and it's yours for the taking. In *The Effective ADHD Parenting Guide,* you will learn:

- What ADHD really looks like, not just the textbook symptoms, but real day-to-day experiences your child faces. It's like finally getting the rulebook for a game you've been playing without instructions.
- How to open the lines of communication, learn to speak and listen in ADHD, a language where words bridge gaps, not create them.
- How to cope with emotional outbursts. With emotional regulation, you'll have a toolkit for staying cool and teaching your child to do the same.
- How to say goodbye to chaos and hello to structure. Find out how a solid routine can be your family's anchor.
- How to build self-esteem, teaching your child to see themselves as the champions they are, quirks and all.
- How to turn academic struggles into opportunities so they prosper in school, not just get by.

This isn't your average, run-of-the-mill advice; it's ADHD-specific. This book gets ADHD. It doesn't slap on a Band-Aid and call it a cure. It hands you strategies that work with ADHD brains. Every tip and every strategy taps into your child's unique potential, not just squashing down the tough stuff. And the best part? The goal is connection, not correction. You're managing behaviors, yes, but you're also nurturing a relationship with strategies for bonding, understanding their world, and guiding them without breaking their spirit.

COMING UP

The first chapter is where you'll start peeling back the layers of the misconceptions and really get why your child ticks the way they do. It's the foundation of everything, understanding that ADHD isn't a one-dimensional challenge but a multifaceted part of their unique blueprint.

UNCOVERING THE LAYERS OF YOUR CHILD'S ADHD

Meet 12-year-old Noah. His teacher assigns a project to build a model of the solar system. While others follow the typical model structure with the sun at the center and planets circling around, Noah thinks differently. He surprises everyone by imagining the entire galaxy, not just our solar system. His model is a colorful whirl of stars, comets, and planets, all buzzing with activity. Noah explains, "Our solar system isn't alone. There's an entire universe out there; why wouldn't I include that?"

Noah's ADHD fuels his outside-the-box thinking. His model, alive with creativity and energy, captures the classroom's imagination. He doesn't just see things as they are but as they could be. This is the vibrant side of ADHD—a mind brimming with energy, enthusiasm, and creativity. Sure, it's different, but different isn't bad. In fact, it can be beautifully unexpected, just like Noah's universe, swirling with endless possibilities.

Isn't it fascinating how a child with ADHD can channel their energy toward creativity and imagination? Now, let's uncover the layers of these vibrant minds, identifying the hallmarks of ADHD to better understand and support them.

STRATEGY 1: RECOGNIZING ADHD SYMPTOMS AND BEHAVIORS

ADHD stands for Attention-Deficit/Hyperactivity Disorder. It's a neurodevelopmental disorder, meaning it's rooted in the brain's structure and functions. It has nothing to do with being lazy, undisciplined, or bad parenting, and it's definitely not a character flaw.

Children with ADHD experience persistent patterns of inattention, hyperactivity, and impulsivity that interfere with functioning or development (NIMH, 2023). These traits will be more frequent and severe compared to the norm. They might struggle with focusing on one task, and their minds might jump from one thought to another like a hyperactive bunny. They might also have a hard time sitting still or curbing impulsive behavior.

Now, you might think, *Well, everyone's like that sometimes.* And you're right. But with ADHD, these behaviors are so severe that they interfere with daily life: think school, home life, family relationships, you name it. One key detail to remember is that ADHD isn't a one-size-fits-all condition. It comes in three types:

- predominantly inattentive
- predominantly hyperactive/impulsive
- combined

Different symptoms are associated with each type, making each person's experience unique.

Here's an interesting tidbit: ADHD isn't just a childhood disorder. Many people continue to experience symptoms into adulthood. And some adults are even diagnosed for the first time later in life (Fairbank, 2023).

ADHD Diagnosis

Receiving a diagnosis is not as simple as taking one test and getting the results. It's more like piecing together a complex puzzle, and several steps and professionals are involved in the process. Typically, you'd start with your primary care doctor. They may refer you to a psychiatrist, psychologist, or a pediatrician who specializes in ADHD. The professionals will conduct a comprehensive evaluation, which includes a clinical interview, a medical exam, and psychological tests (Seay et al., 2019). They'll also gather information like medical, developmental, school, work, and family history. They might also talk to you, the parent or caregiver, other family members, or teachers to see how your child's symptoms manifest in different areas of their life.

Diagnostic criteria for ADHD are outlined in the Diagnostic and Statistical Manual of Mental Disorders (DSM-5) (CDC, 2022). There must be a certain number of symptoms from either (or both) the inattention group or the hyperactivity and impulsivity group. These symptoms must be present before the age of 12, persist for more than six months, and interfere with at least two areas of life (like home or school).

ADHD Causes

Now, onto the causes of ADHD. It's not a result of bad parenting or too much sugar, despite what you might have heard. In fact, it's largely genetic. Research indicates that it's often passed down from parent to child (Vanbuskirk, 2022).

But genetics is only part of the story. Brain structure and function are also contributing. Studies show that people with ADHD have differences in the areas of their brains that control attention and activity (Wilkin, 2023). Certain environmental factors might contribute to ADHD, too (Koseva, 2023). For example, exposure to lead or maternal smoking and alcohol use during pregnancy have been linked to an increased risk of ADHD.

THE DIVERSITY OF ADHD SYMPTOMS

Let's clear up a common misconception: ADHD looks different in everyone. Kids with ADHD present a variety of symptoms, each with its unique spin on the condition.

Take little Omar, for instance. He's the textbook example of hyperactivity. He's always on the move, almost like being driven by a motor. He's the kid who's up and running before the sun rises and the last one to wind down at night. Climbing, jumping, running; if it involves movement, Omar's there. But then there's Chloé. Chloé's ADHD doesn't look like Omar's at all. She's not particularly hyperactive. Instead, she struggles with attention. Keeping focused on one thing at a time is a tall order for her. Even the simplest homework assignment feels like a mountain to climb. Her mind wanders, and before she knows it, she's daydreaming about unicorns instead of working on her math problems.

Then, you have kids like Adrian. His ADHD is more about impulsivity. He often acts before he thinks, making hasty decisions without contemplating all the options. He'll blurt out answers in class without raising his hand or dash across the street without looking both ways. His impulsivity makes it hard for him to wait his turn or to think things through. Let's not forget Sophie, who has a combination of symptoms. She's hyperactive, inattentive, and impulsive. With her, it's a whirlwind of constant movement, daydreaming, and spur-of-the-moment decisions. It's a tough mix, but it's her reality.

There's also a group of kids with ADHD who don't fit the typical mold. They're not hyperactive, they're not impulsive, and they don't have trouble paying attention. Instead, they struggle with executive functioning skills: things like organizing, planning, and prioritizing. They're like Chloé, who struggles to organize her schoolwork or manage her time well.

The point is that ADHD isn't a cookie-cutter condition. Each child with ADHD has a unique mix of symptoms. Omar, Chloé, Adrian, and Sophie all have ADHD, but their experiences are vastly different, and that's okay. It's exactly this diversity we can use to appreciate the complexity of ADHD and to remember that not all kids with ADHD will look or act the same way.

Signs of Inattention:

- **Trouble focusing:** Imagine your child sitting at the dining table with their homework spread out before them. You've explained the task, but 10 minutes later, they're staring out the window, pencil forgotten in hand.
- **Forgetfulness:** Has your child ever forgotten their lunchbox or homework even after reminding them multiple times?

- **Difficulty following instructions:** Say you've asked your child to clean their room. You come back an hour later; the toys are still scattered around, and they're playing with their toy car.
- **Easily distracted:** You're in the park, and your kid is on the swing. But the moment a dog trots by, they're off the swing and chasing after it, forgetting all about the fun they were having.
- **Difficulty in organizing tasks:** Have you ever noticed your child struggling to organize their school bag or decide what to do first? It's like they're confronted with a mountain they don't know how to climb.
- **Avoiding tasks that require sustained effort:** If your child consistently avoids activities that require a steady focus, it could be a telltale sign of ADHD inattention.
- **Daydreaming:** Daydreaming is a part of childhood, but if your child seems to be in their own world more often than not, like during a class or while doing homework, it might be a symptom of ADHD inattention.

Signs of Hyperactivity:

- **Fidgeting:** At dinner time, maybe your child can't seem to sit still, constantly tapping their feet or drumming their fingers on the table.

- **Non-stop talking:** Often interrupting others, they talk incessantly and switch topics rapidly, just like when they describe their day at school, jumping from math class to the playground to their best friend's new pet.
- **Unfinished tasks:** Often leaving tasks unfinished as they quickly lose interest and move on to the next exciting thing. Their bedroom is probably littered with half-finished drawings and toys left mid-play.
- **Constant movement:** They seem to be always "on the go" or "driven by a motor," which can feel like they never tire out, running, jumping, and climbing around.
- **Difficulty playing quietly:** Whether a quiet game of *chess* or reading a book, these activities may be difficult for kids with ADHD. For example, those times when sitting through a game of *Monopoly* without getting restless feels impossible.
- **Frequent interruptions:** They have a hard time waiting their turn to speak. Like when you're talking with them, they interrupt you before you can finish your sentence.

Signs of Impulsivity:

- **Acting without thinking:** Impulsivity means acting on a whim, without any thought for the consequences. Imagine them on the weekend, riding their bike recklessly down a busy street without considering the danger.

- **Intrusiveness:** Personal space isn't a concept your child fully grasps. They often barge into their sibling's room or your office, always eager to join whatever's happening.
- **Being easily distracted:** External stimuli like noises, movement, or objects draw them away from what they're supposed to be concentrating on. They may get easily sidetracked by unrelated thoughts or daydreaming during class.
- **Impatience:** Waiting in line, taking turns, or any form of delayed gratification feels impossible. You've seen it when they're playing and can't wait their turn.
- **Emotional overreactions:** They can get angry or emotional because of minor frustrations or setbacks. Maybe you've seen them burst into tears at the slightest criticism from a teacher.

There are, unfortunately, quite a few myths that can arise from a lack of knowledge about the symptoms of ADHD. Let's now debunk these misconceptions so you can understand ADHD better and support your child (and yourself!) more empathetically. As well as create a more inclusive and supportive environment in which your child can thrive.

MYTH BUSTING

Myths and misconceptions: They're the misunderstandings and stigma that perpetuate stereotypes and prevent everyone with ADHD from receiving the understanding and support they need. Some common myths about ADHD include:

- **Myth 1:** ADHD isn't a real disorder; it's just an excuse for bad behavior.

  - **Fact:** ADHD is a recognized disability that affects the brain's executive functions (Sherman, Numerous studies have provided evidence of structural and differences in ADHD brains compared to those without the disorder (Sinfield, 2022).

- **Myth 2:** Only children have ADHD.

  - **Fact:** While ADHD is commonly diagnosed in childhood, it can persist into adulthood. In fact, around 90% of children with continue to experience symptoms in adulthood (Abdelnour et al., 2022). The symptoms may change over time—hyperactivity tends to decrease—but the core features of inattention, hyperactiv ity, and impulsivity remain (Cherney, 2022).

- **Myth 3:** ADHD is caused by bad parenting.

  - **Fact:** The cause of ADHD is not known. However, environmental factors may influence symptoms without causing the disorder. ADHD is a neurodevelopmental disorder with a strong genetic component (NHS, 2018a). Research has shown that ADHD is highly heritable, with genetic factors accounting for about 80% of the risk (Grimm et al., 2020).

- **Myth 4:** Medication is the only treatment for ADHD.

  - **Fact:** While medication can be an effective treatment option for many ADHD cases, it's not the only approach. A combined treatment plan made up of behavioral therapy, counseling, and lifestyle modifications is often recommended for the best outcomes (NHS, 2018c).

- **Myth 5:** Everyone has a little bit of ADHD.

  - **Fact:** While it is true that most people have issues with attention or impulsivity from time to time, ADHD is characterized by persistent and impairing symptoms that significantly affect day-to-day life (Roggli, 2023). It's not just a minor annoyance or occasional distraction that everyone experiences.

STRATEGY 2: EXPLORING THE NEUROLOGICAL UNDERPINNINGS OF ADHD

Do you know these common misconceptions about ADHD? Well, brace yourself because we're about to debunk them and explore the fascinating world of the neurological underpinnings of ADHD. Turns out, understanding the truth behind these myths provides insight into the intricate connection between our brains and ADHD.

Brain Functioning and Structure

In children with ADHD, the brain functions a little differently compared to those without the disorder.

The Prefrontal Cortex: One key area affected is the prefrontal cortex, which is responsible for executive functions like attention, impulse control, and decision-making (Wilkins, 2023). Structurally, the prefrontal cortex in ADHD children matures more slowly and can also be slightly smaller and less active than in neurotypical children (Cronkleton, 2021). This explains the issues with focusing, organizing tasks, staying on track, and making sound judgments.

The Basal Ganglia: Another area affected is the basal ganglia, a collection of structures deep within the brain involved in motor control, learning, and behavior (Cleveland Clinic, 2022). In children with ADHD, there are abnormalities in the functioning of the basal ganglia, which contribute to their symptoms.

The basal ganglia regulates the release of dopamine, a neurotransmitter responsible for transmitting signals between brain cells, and is involved in the reward and pleasure centers of the brain (Turk et al., 2021). In ADHD, there is a dysregulation of dopamine levels (Johnson, 2019), so when levels are low, the incentive to stay engaged with activities in the long term isn't there. This is because low dopamine interferes with motivation and reward processing. For example, children with ADHD may struggle to feel motivated to complete tasks that don't provide immediate rewards or stimulation. So it's this that makes them procrastinate, show little drive, and struggle to start or finish projects.

Additionally, dopamine helps regulate impulse control and inhibitory responses (Duggal, 2021). When dopamine levels are low, children with ADHD may struggle to control their impulses, leading to impulsive behaviors such as acting without thinking, interrupting others, or engaging in risky activities.

It's not just brain structure and low dopamine that contributes to the behavioral symptoms of ADHD.

The Limbic System: The limbic system is a complex network of brain structures responsible for regulating emotions and behavior. In children with ADHD, the limbic system does not follow an atypical developmental structure (Connaughton et al., 2023). This means they are more prone to emotional dysregulation, leading to anger, frustration, and low frustration tolerance, to name a few (Barkley, 2021).

Additionally, the limbic system is responsible for processing and interpreting emotional cues from the environment (Felton, 2022). Attention and focus problems can make it difficult for children with ADHD to accurately perceive or interpret other people's emotional signals. In response, there may be misinterpretation of social cues, difficulties in recognizing and understanding emotions, and inappropriate emotional responses (Tehrani-Doost et al., 2017).

Now that the ADHD theory is done and dusted, let's get back to what matters: the brain structure differences in children with ADHD have nothing to do with intelligence or character. It simply means that their brains function differently, which manifests as ADHD symptoms. No matter what you hear, know that ADHD children can have varying levels of intelligence and character, just like any other person.

FROM THEORY TO PRACTICE

Understanding the neurological aspects of ADHD in children can totally transform your approach to parenting. You see, ADHD is not just about kids being hyperactive or having trouble focusing; it goes way deeper than that. By looking into the neuroscience behind ADHD, it becomes clearer to figure out how their brains work.

It all comes down to this: Children with ADHD have differences in brain structure and functioning compared to their peers. Their prefrontal cortex, responsible for things like impulse control and attention, doesn't function as efficiently. This means that they struggle with self-regulation and staying on task. When you grasp this, it changes everything. Instead of getting frustrated or thinking your child is intentionally misbehaving, you start to empathize with them. You understand they're not doing it on purpose; it's just their brain is wired differently.

So, what does this mean for your parenting approach? It means being patient, understanding, and flexible. Rather than expecting them to conform to traditional methods, you can tailor your parenting style to them. Things like breaking tasks into smaller, manageable chunks, establishing routines, and providing clear instructions, all while celebrating their small victories and offering them plenty of positive reinforcement. Then, guess what happens? You become a more empathetic and effective parent. You create an environment that meets your child's specific needs, boosting their self-esteem and well-being. So, embrace this knowledge and let it guide you in nurturing your amazing child with ADHD.

COMING UP

Understanding ADHD helps, but it's not enough on its own. Now, let's get into our first strategy: building effective communication. You've already taken the first step by understanding your child's ADHD, and now it's time to unlock the power of communication. Communication strategies go a long way toward connecting with your child, helping them thrive socially, all while establishing a strong support system.

2

BUILDING EFFECTIVE COMMUNICATION

For us, school was where we had the most issues: forgotten homework, missed instructions, you name it. We were at our wits' end, and I knew we needed to break through to him, show him he is heard, and that he matters.

I decided to switch things up and get on his level. I ditched the lectures and the exasperated sighs. Instead, I asked him to tell me about his day, with no interruptions, just him talking and me truly listening. His eyes light up; I guess he wasn't used to being the star of the show. It's not easy to dedicate enough time to him with three other children. But I wanted him to know that he could share his struggles with me so we could work together as a team (just the two of us). The main thing was creating a safe space to talk about things.

After he was done, I repeated some of what he said so he knew I was paying attention. Then, I gently weaved in advice, like tackling homework one piece at a time. Explaining that many of the greatest things in life come from those who aren't necessarily "typical." I'm not talking at him but with him, and it finally clicked.

The change wasn't overnight, but it's there. He started trying those baby steps we talked about. Homework gets done, sometimes even on time! He hates it sometimes, no doubt, but at least he knows we can address any issues together.

There's this new thing in his eyes now, too—confidence. We're connecting, and it's like we've unlocked this whole new level in our relationship. He knows I have his back for any small or big things.

STRATEGY 3: ACTIVE LISTENING TECHNIQUES

Active listening: You've probably heard the term, but what is it? Take a moment to imagine someone not only hearing your words but really tuning in to what you're saying, catching every nuance, and understanding the emotions behind the words. That's active listening.

Now, why's it a game-changer? For starters, it builds trust like nothing else (Jackson, 2023). When someone actively listens to you, it's validating, right? You feel respected and valued. More than just nodding along; it's engaging with what you're saying, asking questions, and giving feedback to show they're in the moment with you. Let's say you're hashing something out with a friend, and they're actively listening. You're more likely to open up, share more, and get to the heart of things, turning a basic chat into a real connection.

It's not just personal; it's professional gold, too. Managers, teammates, salespeople: Anyone can harness active listening to improve collaboration, solve problems faster, and avoid misunderstandings.

Active Listening and ADHD

Active listening when it comes to a child with ADHD? It's not just important; it's essential. You're dealing with a kid who's got a Ferrari engine for a brain with bicycle brakes. Imagine that for a second. They're going a mile a minute, thoughts racing, and here's where you come in with active listening.

First off, you're giving them a rare gift: your full, undivided attention. This is huge because these kids often get the "not now" or "I'm busy" treatment, not necessarily by you, but by society as a whole. By actively listening, you're showing them they matter, their opinions matter, and this makes a huge difference to their self-esteem because you're validating their experiences, which makes them feel heard and understood, contributing to a stronger sense of self-worth and confidence (Adejokun, 2020).

But there's more. ADHD brains can have a hard time processing and expressing thoughts in an orderly way. When you actively listen, you're helping them untangle those thoughts; you're patient, you're asking clarifying questions, and you're giving them space to explore their ideas without bias. This can lead to some real lightbulb moments for them.

Response-wise, active listening helps you get to the root of what's going on. Maybe there's a meltdown in the park, and instead of trying to shush it, you're there, listening to what's behind the tantrum. It helps you respond more thoughtfully and calm them down because you've got the full picture, not just the emotional outburst. When children with ADHD are stressed or overwhelmed, their bodies release cortisol, activating the fight-or-flight response which restricts access to their prefrontal cortex —the part of the brain responsible for rational thinking and emotional regulation (Schultz, 2023). They're literally unable to calm themselves down. But by actively listening during a meltdown, you give them a safe space to express their emotions, reducing cortisol levels and allowing their prefrontal cortex to recover.

Active Listening Techniques

With active listening, in addition to managing behaviors in a better manner, you're developing a deep, empathetic understanding. For a kid with ADHD, having someone who really listens and supports them along the way can make all the difference toward a stronger connection. This is what it looks like:

- **Eye contact:** Looking directly at them when they're speaking to show your full attention.
- **Nodding:** Gently nodding your head to indicate understanding and encouragement, letting them know you're engaged in the conversation.
- **Verbal acknowledgments:** Use phrases like "I see," "That's interesting," or "Tell me more" to let them know you're listening and interested in what they have to say.
- **Reflective statements:** Repeating or paraphrasing what they've said to demonstrate your understanding and to clarify any misunderstandings.
- **Open-ended questions:** Ask questions that need more than a simple "yes" or "no" answer, encouraging them to express their thoughts and feelings in more detail.
- **Summarizing:** Recapping the main points of the conversation to establish mutual understanding and show that you're paying attention.
- **Avoid interrupting:** Letting them express themselves without interruption, giving them space to share their thoughts.

Now, while these techniques sound easy enough in theory, they're not so simple in practice, are they?

Communicating with kids who have ADHD comes with a unique set of hurdles. Eye contact, for one, can be a tricky thing. You might think they're not paying attention if they're not looking you in the eye, but that's not always the case. These kids often struggle to hold eye contact because it demands a level of focus that can be super taxing for their brains (Raza, 2022). It doesn't mean their ears are closed off.

Another thing is their energy levels. They can be off the charts, right? Sitting still for a conversation isn't their strong suit, and they might interrupt or change subjects like channel surfing. It's not that they're not interested in what you're saying; their minds are just bouncing around a bunch of thoughts at once.

Plus, emotional regulation? That's a steep hill to climb for them. When you chat, they might get frustrated or upset more easily, but it's not a reflection of your communication skills. They're just processing things differently and might need more time to digest things and respond to you.

So, when talking to your child, remember, they're probably listening, even if it doesn't look like it by typical standards. They process and show engagement differently. What we need to do is figure out how to tune into their unique frequency and turn the static into a clear channel. Let's shift gears and lay out some custom active listening cues that click with their distinct needs, transforming communication hurdles into a smooth two-way street.

TEACH ACTIVE LISTENING CUES

For those times when you feel like you're speaking a different language when trying to get your ADHD child to listen, teaching them listening cues is like unlocking the secret code to communication. It's your superpower in the battle of attention spans.

- Snag their attention with a calm, friendly cue; think of a gentle touch on the shoulder, or use their name before you chat. Eye contact can be tricky, so instead of insisting they stare you down, encourage them to look at your nose or forehead; it's less intense but still creates a connection.
- Mimic their energy level; if they're hyped, keep your vibe upbeat. When they speak, lean in, nod, and toss in the occasional "uh-huh" to show you're with them. If they drift off topic, gently steer them back with an "I see, and what about...?" Keep your sentences short and sweet, and chunk down instructions; this isn't the time for a monologue.
- If you've got a point to make, use visuals like simple drawings or gestures to anchor your words. And here's the scoop: practice the "pause." After you say something, give them a moment to

take it all in. It's like a mini-break for their brain to catch up and process.

- For something specific to talk about, grab their attention before you start talking; use their name and make sure they're looking in your general direction. Eye contact isn't everything, as long as they're tuned in. Try saying, "Hey Claire, let's chat about your science homework."

- Don't forget to acknowledge the good stuff. When they nail that eye contact or stay on topic, let them know it's a big deal. Positive reinforcement works wonders.

- Keep things interactive, too. Throw in a "What do you think about that?" or "Can you tell me more?" It's like tossing a ball back and forth; it keeps them engaged. If they're fidgeting, don't stress. They might still be listening, but to check in, saying something like, "Show me with your hands, how big was that frog you saw?"

- Break down your talk into bite-sized pieces; ADHD minds can get overstimulated by too much information (Maynard, 2021). Say, "First, we'll do your homework, and then it's playtime," rather than giving a full day's schedule in one go.

- Staying on track can be tough, so guide them back gently if they veer off. "That's a cool story, Bobby, but let's finish talking about your homework first, okay?"

- Don't forget to model what you teach. Nod while they talk and repeat some points they make, like, "So you're saying the frog was green with spots? Interesting!" It shows you're listening and gives them a live demo to mirror.

Consistency is key with these cues. Just keep at them and soon enough, you'll see your child's active listening skills start to shine.

Practice Active Listening With Your Child

Okay, so you've got your active listening techniques under your belt. Plus, you know exactly what cues you need to give to get them to listen. You're in the middle of a conversation, and suddenly, you whip out your active listening skills like a secret weapon. But wait! Without giving them a heads-up, it could catch them off guard and make things confusing for them, especially if this is new to them. So, you need to let them know you're about to use these techniques and the ones to follow.

1. Start by saying, "Hey, Shaun, I want to try something new during our chat today. It's called active listening, and it'll help us understand each other better. Is that cool with you?" It's always a good idea to explain the purpose and ask for their consent. This way, you're creating a spirit of collaboration and making them feel involved.

2. Let them know your intention is not to punish them but to improve communication and make things less overwhelming for them in all areas of their life. You can say, "I just want you to know, Shaun, that this isn't about you being in trouble or anything like that. It's actually because I care about what you have to say, and I want us to have even better conversations. So, we're making things even more awesome between us. Sound good?" By reassuring them that active listening is about growth and understanding, you create a safe and supportive environment for open dialogue.

3. Next, share some simple guidelines (from the active listening techniques listed above), like maintaining eye contact, nodding or using affirmations, and avoiding interruptions. Use examples to illustrate, like, "When you're speaking, I'll focus on you, and when I'm speaking, you'll focus on me, like when we watched that exciting movie together."

Exercises and Activities to Improve Listening Skills

Practicing active listening through fun exercises and activities is like turning a routine chat into a game. It's a win-win! You get to channel their energy into something positive while sneaking in some killer communication skills. They'll learn to tune in, and you will both enjoy quality time without the eye-rolls. Plus, it's a sneaky way to boost their focus and self-esteem. They'll feel heard and valued, and you'll get to actually finish a sentence.

- **Emotion charades:** Grab some cards and write down different emotions on each. Take turns drawing a card and acting out the emotion without speaking. The listener has to guess the emotion, teaching them to pick up on non-verbal cues.
- **Storytelling time:** Take turns telling short stories, each person adding a sentence or two. You don't have to be Stephen King for this; you can use anything you like, "What I did in school today," or "A day in the life of…" This is a great technique to encourage active listening, as you must pay attention to what the other person is saying to continue the story.
- **Mirror, mirror:** Sit facing each other and take turns mimicking each other's facial expressions and gestures based on a specific emotion. Make sure to name the emotion to encourage focused observation and attentive listening to capture the nuances of nonverbal communication.
- **Repeat after me:** Share a fun fact or story with your child, then have them repeat back the main points. This encourages them to listen for key details.

- **Sound detective:** Go on a sound scavenger hunt around the house or outdoors. Get them to close their eyes and listen carefully to identify different sounds. They'll learn to listen attentively and distinguish between various noises.
- **I Spy listening edition:** Play a modified version of I Spy, where you describe sounds instead of objects. For example, "I spy with my little ear, something that sounds like birds chirping." This activity hones their auditory perception and listening skills.

Top these off with a little positive reinforcement to let them know they've done a good job getting involved. Things don't always have to go to plan; just know that the more time you spend teaching them how to listen, you're making the experience engaging and enjoyable. So, when the time comes when you need them to listen, they'll have a better idea of what's expected of them.

There's no doubt about it: Active listening strengthens the connection between you and your child. But it also lays the foundation for understanding their nonverbal messages. Suddenly, you're more in tune with their body language, facial expressions, and tone of voice, picking up on subtle gestures, allowing you to grasp their emotions and needs beyond words.

STRATEGY 4: UNDERSTANDING NONVERBAL CUES AND COMMUNICATION STRATEGIES

Nonverbal cues are the subtle, unspoken ways we communicate to others without using words. It's like a secret language of gestures, facial expressions, body movements, and even the tone of our voice. While words express our thoughts, nonverbal cues reveal our unconscious emotions, intentions, and attitudes (Segal et al., 2023).

Say you're talking to someone, but their crossed arms and furrowed brow tells you they're not quite on board. Or when a friend's bright smile and open posture show their excitement and interest in a conversation. These nonverbal cues provide valuable insights into how others feel and what they're really thinking. There's no doubt that nonverbal cues are powerful tools in communication, often conveying messages that words alone cannot capture. They can indicate confidence or nervousness, agreement or disagreement, sincerity or deception. From a firm handshake to a reassuring pat on the back, nonverbal cues add depth and richness to our interactions.

Non-Verbal Cues and ADHD

Understanding non-verbal cues in your ADHD child will go a long way in improving your communication strategies. This is because interacting with a child with ADHD requires a unique approach, one that relies heavily on nonverbal communication. In situations when they're overwhelmed or struggling to express themselves verbally, nonverbal cues bridge the gap between frustration and empathy. For example:

- If they're fidgeting or tapping their foot like a woodpecker during a homework session, maybe over a tough math problem or the sheer amount of tasks, it may indicate stress or anxiety. By picking up on this cue, you can swoop in with support before it escalates into a meltdown or shutdown.
- Or at a noisy birthday party, they're tugging at their collar like it's suddenly turned into sandpaper; it might not be the tag but a sensory overload. That's your cue to help them avoid an overwhelming spiral by finding a quiet corner or suggesting a breather outside.

Nonverbal communication also helps in creating a positive and nurturing environment. Let's say your child reaches a milestone, like tying their shoelaces for the first time. Instead of congratulating them with words, you celebrate their success with a high-five, a hug, or a big smile. These nonverbal gestures reinforce their accomplishment and boost self-esteem (Raising Children, 2017). The cherry on top is how nonverbal cues assist with redirecting and managing challenging behaviors (Vierstra, 2023). Let's say your child becomes agitated during a family outing. A gentle touch or a soft voice can help them regulate their emotions and guide them toward a more peaceful state.

These nonverbal cues are the breadcrumbs taking you into their inner world. When you're tuned in and responding, you're dodging a potential crisis while building a bridge between understanding and trust, the ultimate parenting win! Now, onto deciphering them.

INTERPRET AND RESPOND TO YOUR CHILD'S NONVERBAL CUES

Interpreting and responding to these nonverbal cues is like being a detective in a silent film; you've got to pay attention to the actions because they speak louder than words. Each cue is a chance to connect and support your child, turning everyday moments into solid gold parenting.

- They're scrunching their face more than a detective pondering a mystery. That might not only be a quirky expression; it's a sign they're confused or stuck on something. Don't wait for them to verbalize it; ask them what's up. Offer to break down the problem or give an example to ease their mental cramp.

- Suddenly, in the middle of a group activity, they're as still as a statue while everyone buzzes around. That might not be them being rude or uninterested; they're possibly just overwhelmed and can't find an entry point into the chaos. Here's your cue: Guide them with a gentle suggestion like, "Why don't you join the game of tag?" or "How about you and I start our own drawing over here?"

- Have you ever noticed them avoiding eye contact, not out of disrespect, but because they're trying to concentrate on your words? Eye contact can be super intense for ADHD brains, so give them the space to listen in their own way. Maybe they focus better while doodling or looking at a fixed object; it's all good as long as they absorb the conversation.

- With other people around, you notice them fidgeting with their shirt hem like it's a puzzle to solve; they're not just playing with their clothes; they're likely feeling anxious or uncomfortable. Maybe they're gearing up to ask a question or need to use the bathroom but are too embarrassed to ask. Give them a reassuring nod or a quick, discreet check-in to help them feel seen and supported.

- This will help them snap back to the moment and engage without feeling lost or embarrassed.
- Seeing them chewing on their pencil isn't just a bad habit; it could be a sign they need a sensory break or are struggling to focus. Instead of scolding, consider offering a stress ball or a chewable necklace or bracelet. These are products specially designed for sensory outlet and work by redirecting the need to chew into something less destructive and more helpful for concentration.

Spotting and responding to these nonverbal hints do more than keep the peace. They assist your child to make sense of their world with your understanding as their superpower. Every gesture or look is a valuable clue into what they're experiencing, and your role is to be the translator and guide, helping them find their footing one cue at a time.

Once you've got a handle on your child's nonverbal cues, like that foot-tapping SOS when they're stuck, you're already a step ahead in the communication dance. Now, let's turn the tables and help them tune into verbal cues because catching the subtle pitch in your voice when you're pleased, or the speed-up when you're anxious can dramatically transform how they connect with others.

Teach Your Child to Identify Verbal Cues

Teaching your ADHD child to pick up on verbal cues is like handing them the secret code to human interactions. When they learn to listen for changes in tone, pace, and volume, they're unlocking context clues that reveal emotions and intentions behind words, like understanding sarcasm or detecting boredom. This skill is a game-changer for them; it means they can adapt their behavior to fit the vibe of a conversation, avoid misunderstandings, and respond in a manner understood by others.

- **Tone of voice:** Play a game where you say the same sentence in different ways and have them guess if you're excited, annoyed, or joking.
- **Volume:** Say you're reading a story; switch it up by whispering when the plot sneaks around a secret, or boom your voice during a big reveal. This shows them that loud equals importance or excitement, and quiet could mean serious or sneaky.
- **Pace:** Speed up your chatter when you're pretending to be in a hurry and watch them connect the dots that fast talk can mean stress or excitement. Slow it down to show seriousness or sadness. It's about matching your speech to the emotion, like a soundtrack to a movie scene, so

they learn to listen not just to the words but the music behind them.

- **Pause:** Teach them that when someone stops mid-sentence, it's often a sign they're unsure or expecting a response. Encourage your child to jump in with a question or a comment to keep the chat flowing. It's like teaching them to hit the gas pedal when the conversation hits a yellow light, keeping it cruising along smoothly.
- **Sarcasm and jokes:** Next time you joke, lay it on thick with a wink or a nudge. They'll start noticing that a funny tone means you're not serious. It's like giving them a wink with words, and soon, they'll be winking back with their own well-timed jokes.
- **Use real-life examples:** Here, teach them to hear beyond the words to the emotion wrapped around them, like peeling back layers to find the real message hidden inside.

  - When their sibling says "fine" with a stomp, point out that "fine" isn't just fine; it's frustrating.
  - After losing a game, their friend mutters, "Whatever," with an eye roll. That's your cue to lean in and whisper to them, "See that? 'Whatever' isn't a brush-off; there's disappointment behind those words."

○ When watching a movie, a character says, "Nothing's wrong," but they're clenching their jaw or making it obvious in some other passive way. They're not happy. Pause the scene and make it a teachable moment. "Look at that jaw or see the disappointment in their face. They're not being honest when they say "nothing's wrong," that's anger trying to stay hidden. It'll be like you're both detectives, deciphering the secret code of body language together.

How to Communicate During a Meltdown

Nailing those verbal and non-verbal cues with your child sets up a solid base for when things get heated, but they're also the anchor in the emotional throes of a meltdown. Recognizing the shift from calm to stormy means you can throw that anchor down fast, keeping communication lines from snapping when it gets rough.

- Lean down to their level, lock eyes gently, and drop your voice to a whisper; it may seem counterintuitive, but it works. You're not shushing them; you're a narrator of a calm story, where your soft tone is the main character. Soft and quiet tones help their brain tune in to the quiet, pushing out the noise of the meltdown.

- o Let's say they're upset because they can't get past the "final boss" scene in their computer game. Instead of saying, "It's just a game," which might rile them up more, try (in a whisper to pull them back to curiosity and away from the edge), "Wow, you put a lot of effort into trying to beat him, and it's tough to see it end like that. Let's take a deep breath and try again when you've had some time to think about what to do next." Your acknowledgment makes them feel seen, and the breathing gives both of you a reset button.

- For strategy, think of a distraction, not a diversion. If they're spiraling because they can't get their shoes on right, offer to race them to see who can tie their laces faster. It's not avoiding the problem; it's redirecting their focus to something fun, which can break the spell of a meltdown.
- Use simple, direct language with clear choices. Say they're melting down over homework. Avoid "Do you want to continue?" because it's too open-ended. Go for "Do you want to do math or reading first?" It gives them control without overwhelming them.
- Validate their feelings with empathy, but keep it brief. Mid-meltdown, they're not able to process anything, so keep things short and to the point. Try "I see you're upset because it's bedtime.

Bedtime is boring for us all (even if it isn't for you), so let's pick a book to wind down with." Short, sweet, and you're moving them toward a solution.

- Always be the model of calm. They'll pick up on that serene vibe if you're a duck on water. Even if you're paddling like mad below the surface, keep your exterior smooth. It's the calm composure that says, "We've got this, no matter how bad things get."

COMING UP

When you've got the communication to dance down with your child—knowing when to lead with a question or follow with a pause—you're setting the stage for better social skills. Yet, how can you make your new strategy playbook even more valuable? Enhance it with strategies that help you call the right shots. And just like that, you're not just managing emotional outbursts but coaching resilience and modulating behavior, one deep breath and choice word at a time.

3

MANAGING EMOTIONAL OUTBURSTS AND BEHAVIORAL CHALLENGES

I t was a busy afternoon at the park, just like any other day. Richard and Suzie, being parents to an ADHD daughter named Mia, know that they can't always predict when meltdowns will strike. But they've learned how to handle them. Each day is a new challenge, and they've realized that while their strategies may not always work perfectly, some days are more successful than others.

In this particular instance, Mia got overwhelmed by the loud noises and the hustle and bustle of the park. She couldn't handle it and started screaming and throwing sand at other kids. Richard and Suzie felt a mix of emotions: embarrassment, frustration, and concern for Mia's well-being. However, they quickly assessed the situation and put their learned strategies into action.

Approaching Mia calmly, they used various techniques to help her regain control. Suzie de-escalated the situation with soft and reassuring words to redirect Mia's attention ("I'm so proud of you for taking deep breaths, and yes, it's very busy today, mommy and daddy think so, too.") Richard used positive reinforcement, praising her for calming down and acknowledging her feelings ("I understand it's frustrating. Let's take a break and find a quiet spot to sit together. We're right here with you, and we'll figure this out.") They also set clear boundaries by explaining to Mia that throwing sand was not acceptable and discussing alternative ways for her to express her frustration. They even proposed a new rule; when feeling angry, she could squeeze her stress ball or count to 10, but throwing things was off-limits. They also emphasized the importance of apologizing to the other children involved.

As Mia gradually calmed down, Suzie and Richard felt a wave of relief wash over them. They were not only relieved but also proud, proud of themselves and proud of Mia. By staying calm, providing support, and teaching her valuable skills, they knew they had handled the outburst well. It gave them hope and reassurance that their strategies were making a positive impact on Mia's emotional regulation and behavior.

STRATEGY 5: POSITIVE REINFORCEMENT AND ENCOURAGEMENT

Have you ever wondered how professional trainers manage to get animals to perform incredible tricks? Or how parents can shape their kids' behavior without resorting to harsh punishments? It all comes down to a psychological concept called positive reinforcement.

Positive reinforcement is a method that encourages desirable behavior and discourages the bad by offering rewards. It's like saying, "Good job! Here's a treat!" to a dog that's just performed a trick correctly. This concept is rooted in a theory called operant conditioning, developed by the renowned psychologist B.F. Skinner. The key element of this approach involves rewarding good behavior with something nice. This makes the behavior more likely to occur again in the future (McLeod, 2023). For example:

- A teacher rewards a student with a gold star for turning in homework on time. The student feels encouraged and, as a result, is more likely to repeat this behavior to receive another gold star.
- A parent is trying to teach their child to put away their toys without fussing. Every time they do it without fussing, they reward their child with something they know they'll enjoy. This acts as a positive reward for good behavior and increases

the likelihood of them repeating the good behavior. Over time, the child associates putting away toys with getting something nice and is more likely to do it even without the reward.

Countless research studies have shown that positive reinforcement works wonders in encouraging desired behaviors in children, especially those diagnosed with ADHD (Leahy, 2021). Because they struggle with controlling impulsive thoughts and regulating their emotions, positive reinforcement guides them into understanding what healthy and productive behaviors look like in action.

Let's say your child finds it difficult to focus on homework. Instead of reprimanding them for being distracted, try rewarding them when they manage to concentrate for a few minutes. The reward could be as simple as words of praise, a favorite snack, or extra playtime. This approach not only motivates them to repeat the behavior but also boosts their self-esteem and confidence (Van De Hey, 2023). Rewards for a job well done send a positive message that their hard work is recognized and valued. This recognition and praise boosts their self-esteem by reinforcing the belief that they can focus and achieve success, leading to increased confidence in their abilities.

The key to success with positive reinforcement is consistency and patience. You can't expect miracles overnight; it's a gradual process, but the outcomes are truly rewarding. It also goes without saying that you should keep the reinforcement realistic and manageable; you don't want to promise a trip to Disneyland every time your child finishes their homework! Instead, consider the following strategies for a more grounded approach.

Verbal Praise

Words carry immense power; a simple "Well done" or "I'm proud of you" goes a long way in encouraging anyone! Children with ADHD often struggle to understand the consequences of their actions (NHS, 2018b), so verbal praise is one of the best ways to manage their emotional outbursts and behavioral challenges. It also reduces the risk of meltdowns by creating a positive environment where children feel recognized and appreciated based on the immediate feedback that verbal praise provides. Here's a step-by-step guide on how to use this method effectively.

Step 1: Identify the Desired Behavior

For verbal praise to be effective, you need to identify the behaviors you want to encourage so your reinforcement is targeted and effective. Random or indiscriminate praise is confusing and may inadvertently reinforce undesirable behaviors. So, know exactly what positive behavior you want to encourage. This could be anything from completing homework on time to helping around the house or behaving well in public.

Step 2: Provide Immediate Praise

Once you've defined the desired behavior, and when they exhibit it, you'll need to provide immediate praise; instant feedback helps them associate the praise with the specific action. For example, if they finish their homework without any prodding, say something like, "Great job on finishing your homework on your own! I knew you could do it!"

Step 3: Be Specific With Your Praise

Generic praise won't always do the trick. Children with ADHD have a hard time understanding ambiguous feedback since they have difficulty regulating their emotions and comprehending abstract ideas. Instead, be specific about what they did well. For instance, if they've tidied their room, rather than saying "Good job," say, "I really appreciate how you've arranged your toys neatly and made your bed. Your room looks great!"

Step 4: Be Genuine and Consistent

Children, especially those with ADHD, are intuitive and can sense insincerity (Neuropsychology, 2020). Consequently, make sure your praise is genuine and consistent. If they've put in effort but haven't quite nailed it, recognize it anyway. You could say, "I see you've been working hard on this, and I appreciate your effort!"

Rewarding Good Behavior

Every time your child nails it—maybe they've sat through a whole dinner without bouncing off their seat, or they've hammered out their math homework without a detour to Distraction Town you've got a direct path to positive reinforcement.

Kids with ADHD aren't short on smarts or creativity; they just need a bit more oomph to channel their energies in the right direction. So, when you catch them being good, make it count. Give a high-five, offer a big thumbs-up, or dish out an extra 15 minutes of screen time. It's like a mental sticky note that says, "Hey, what you just did? Do that again." These rewards do double duty. Not only are you cheering on the good stuff, but you're also gently steering them away from the no-go zones without the fuss. It's like they're collecting bonus points for the behaviors you want to see on repeat. Before you know it, they're not just managing their emotions and impulses better; they're building self-esteem and the kind of habits that stick, even when the rewards aren't front and center.

Don't stop keeping it upbeat, with consistent rewards that are fresh and surprising. You're not just managing behavior; you're nurturing a whole set of life skills that'll turn those "Yes!" moments into the norm.

Step 1: Identify the Behavior

Pinpoint exactly what you want to see more of. Is it listening to you, being quiet during movie night, or not going into full-on meltdown mode when they're frustrated? Be clear and specific because vague goals can be challenging for kids with ADHD to grasp.

Step 2: Choose the Right Reward

Pick something that'll make their eyes light up. It could be extra screen time, a favorite treat, or a special one-on-one activity with you. Keep the reward small but exciting; you want them to be motivated, not overwhelmed or over-stimulated.

Step 3: Set Clear Expectations

Sit down with them and lay out what behaviors you're looking for, when you expect to see them, and what the rewards will be. Clarity is your best friend here.

Step 4: Start Small

Break it down. If you're aiming for an hour of focused homework, start with rewarding 15 minutes of concentration and build from there, then gradually increase the time.

Step 5: Implement the Reward System

Be consistent; every time they display good behavior, they get the reward. No ifs, ands, or buts. Consistency cements the connection between the behavior and the reward.

Step 6: Offer Immediate Rewards

Hand out that high-five, verbal praise, or snack right after the good behavior. The quicker the reward follows the action, the stronger the link.

- Catch them being good, too, because positive reinforcement isn't just about structured rewards; it's also about spontaneous praise. When you see them doing something right, acknowledge it right then and there.

Step 7: Celebrate the Wins, No Matter How Small

Every bit of progress deserves a whoop and a cheer. This keeps motivation and spirits lifted.

Step 8: Gradually Increase Expectations

As they get the hang of it, up the ante. Extend the focus time for that homework or add another layer of complexity to the behavior you want to see. For example, if they're using calming techniques when overwhelmed, ask them to communicate, either verbally or otherwise, what they're thinking and feeling.

- This'll be a double win because you're encouraging emotional regulation and promoting communication and self-awareness.

Step 9: Phase Out the Rewards

Eventually, start to dial back the tangible rewards. The goal is for the good behavior to become a habit, not something they do only for the goodies.

Step 10: Keep Communicating

Sit down with your child regularly to talk about how things are going. Celebrate the wins, and if something isn't working, tweak the system. Maybe they're bored of the rewards, or the goals are too easy or too hard, adjust as needed.

Behavior Chart

A behavior chart is like a scoreboard for your kid's daily wins. It's a vibrant, easy-to-read tracker that maps out specific behaviors you're cheering for, stuff like communicating or listening without a fuss. You're not just telling them what to do; you're showing them, with a colorful chart breaking down their goals into sticker-sized steps.

So why is this gold for kids with ADHD? Simple. Their brains are like pinball machines, with thoughts zipping and bouncing all over. A visual chart cuts through the noise, giving them clear visual cues to follow and gilding them toward the behavior you want to see. Plus, these charts tap into their love for immediate rewards (Editors, 2022). They finish a task, and they get a sticker or a star; instant gratification! It's a way to say, "Hey, I see you, and you're doing awesome," without always using words.

Step 1: Craft It Together

Grab some markers, stickers, or whatever gets them excited and craft that chart together. Personalize it! This makes it fun and gives them a sense of ownership.

- **Choose the chart:** A simple poster board or a printed template.
- **Decide on behaviors:** Pick three to five behaviors you want to encourage. Keep them positive and clear, like *I complete my homework, I pack my backpack without forgetting anything, and I talk to Mom and Dad when I'm feeling angry/upset/overwhelmed.*
- **Set the rewards:** Decide on small, immediate rewards and large, long-term ones. Think of extra screen time or a weekend outing.

Step 2: The Rules of the Game

Now, make it official. Sit down with your little one and lay down the laws of the land.

- **Explain the chart:** Be clear about how it works. "When you do X, you get a sticker. And for X amount of stickers, you'll get something nice to celebrate your hard work."

- **Discuss the rewards:** Make sure they're drooling over the rewards. It's got to be something they'll leap for.
- **Hang it high:** Put the chart somewhere visible, like the fridge door or their bedroom.

Step 3: Using the Chart

This is where the magic happens. Your eagle eyes need to spot those good behaviors and reward them on the spot.

- **Immediate recognition:** The second you see the effort gone into concentrating on their homework or that prolonged eye contact when you're talking to them, get them to put a sticker on the chart.
- **Stay positive:** No sticker for misbehaving; the chart is all about the good vibes.
- **Keep it consistent:** Every time the behavior is done, the reward follows.

Step 4: Their Chart, Their Pride

This chart is as much theirs as it is yours.

- **Let them place stickers:** It's like giving them the key to the kingdom.
- **Track progress together:** Have regular check-ins to admire their sticker collection.
- **Update the chart:** As they master behaviors, add new ones. Keep it fresh!

Step 5: The Rewards

Cashing in on those hard-earned stickers is like hitting the jackpot.

- **Immediate gratification:** Let them bask in the glory of their small rewards often.
- **Grand prize:** Build up to something grand; this is the light at the end of the tunnel.
- **Non-material rewards**: Visual praise or a proud smile are still some of the best rewards.

Step 6: Troubleshooting

Not working? Don't toss the chart just yet.

- **Reassess behaviors:** Maybe they're too vague or too tough. Fine-tune them.
- **Switch-up rewards:** Maybe the carrot at the end of the stick isn't tempting enough.
- **Stay patient:** Rome wasn't built in a day, and neither is perfect behavior.

SETTING CLEAR, ACHIEVABLE GOALS

Positive reinforcement can be an effective strategy for managing emotional outbursts and behavioral challenges, but it needs to be obvious. This means the desired behavior or goal should be clear and easily understood. Kids with ADHD can get easily overwhelmed and without a target in sight, positive reinforcement becomes a shot in the dark. If you tell them, "Let's work on staying calm today," what does "calm" look like to a seven-year-old who can't sit still or focus?

When using positive reinforcement, you need to make sure they know exactly what they're working toward and what behavior will be rewarded. Break it down and say, "If you can stop screaming and throwing things with just three reminders, we'll shoot some hoops (or whatever they enjoy doing) together." That's a goal as clear as a sunny day. They now have a tangible finish line, not a vague concept, and when they reach it, the praise you give is tied directly to a specific achievement. It's not just a pat on the back; it's a message that says, "You did exactly what we aimed for. Great job!" This clarity helps them understand the cause-and-effect relationship between their actions and the rewards, making the positive reinforcement method more effective in managing their behavior. Each little triumph is a confidence builder, and for a child with ADHD, that's like gold. They start to think, "Hey, I've got this," and before you know it, they're managing those emotional hurricanes better, one small win at a time.

Staying Positive and Being Realistic

The concept is simple; using positive reinforcement for desired behavior is like giving your kid their very own game plan. It makes the expectations crystal clear, lights up their reward center, and keeps them focused on the prize. It's not just about keeping them in line; it's about empowering them to connect the dots between actions and outcomes and building those positive habits step by step, all the while having a bit of fun.

Don't let the occasional failure or slow progress discourage you when using positive reinforcement. Sometimes, it takes time for new habits to stick, especially for kids with ADHD who struggle with consistency. Ultimately, positive reinforcement is for creating a supportive environment that focuses on progress, not perfection. Think of it like planting seeds in a garden; you don't expect every seed to sprout instantly or all at once. Some take longer to grow, and others need extra care. It's the same with positive reinforcement; each time you reinforce a desired behavior; you're planting a seed of change in your child's mind.

Even if it doesn't work right away, keep at it. Consistency is key. Stick to your positive reinforcement strategies, and over time, you'll start to see those seeds sprout. Small victories count, and they build momentum. So, stay patient, stay positive, and celebrate every step forward, no matter how small. You're making a difference, even if it doesn't seem like that when you're in the thick of it.

STRATEGY 6: ESTABLISHING CLEAR BOUNDARIES AND CONSISTENT RULES

Do you know how your GPS gives you clear directions to reach your destination? That's what clear boundaries and consistent rules do for kids with ADHD. They need that roadmap to navigate their day-to-day. Everything is fast-paced and buzzing in their world, and without solid boundaries, they can feel adrift in a swamp of stimuli, not knowing which way to tread.

Clear boundaries and rules offer structure that's like a life jacket for them. It keeps them afloat, keeps them safe. They're predictable in nature and create an environment where kids can focus and understand what's expected of them. This predictability reduces anxiety and confusion, which is a big deal because when kids are less anxious, they can focus more (Koseva, 2023a). Consistent rules also teach self-discipline, a skill that'll pay off for a lifetime. Every time they follow a rule, they're flexing their self-control muscles, getting stronger in the process. And when the rules are the same day in and day out, it makes them feel safe and more likely to stick to them. It's like muscle memory. Plus, when kids know the boundaries and what's within the lines, they also learn about natural consequences (O'Donnell, 2018). They start connecting the dots: *If I do this, that happens,* and it's empowering. They realize they have control over what they do and what happens, and it's this autonomy that'll boost their self-esteem big time (Borba, 2022). So, how can you go about it in a way your child can understand?

- **Simple and easy to understand:** Use clear and concise language that leaves no room for ambiguity. For example, instead of saying, "Behave well," you can say, "Use inside voices and keep hands to yourself."
- **Be consistent**: They thrive on routine and structure, so it's important to establish a predictable environment. Stick to the same rules and consequences every time so they know what to expect.
- **Explain the reasons:** Sometimes, they may struggle with impulse control and understanding cause and effect. To counter this, explain why certain behaviors are not allowed while others are. Then, you're helping them develop self-control and make better decisions.
- **Get them involved:** This instills a sense of ownership and responsibility in them. Sit down together and discuss which behaviors are acceptable and what the consequences are if they're not followed; collaboration promotes understanding and cooperation (Padayichie, 2023).
- **Be patient and flexible:** It's easy to forget because ADHD is like a different processing system, so it might not be easy to adjust. Allow for mistakes,

provide gentle reminders, and adjust the rules and consequences as needed based on their child's progress and ADHD traits, which may differ from day to day.

The Role of Consistency in Rule Enforcement

When it comes to enforcing rules, keeping things consistent can make a huge difference in the behavior and development of children with ADHD (*Psychology Today*, 2023). Let's look at why.

Consistency provides a clear and predictable framework for children with ADHD. You reduce the issues with impulsivity and lack of focus by creating a structured environment that teaches boundaries and self-discipline (Schrader, 2023). Imagine if you set a rule that your child needs to complete their homework before watching TV. If you enforce this rule consistently, they'll come to understand there are certain expectations they need to meet before indulging in leisure activities. They'll also learn to understand the consequences of their actions if you reward good behavior and discourage negative behaviors.

When it comes to managing ADHD-related challenges, consistency extends beyond rules and consequences; it also applies to routines and schedules. Establishing consistent routines for daily activities like meals, bedtime, and homework promotes stability and helps them manage their time and responsibilities better. For example, having a set bedtime routine with consistent steps like brushing teeth, reading or listening to a book, or any activities that promote relaxation, and going to bed at the same time each night regulates their sleep patterns, which in turn has a positive effect on their behavior and attention span during the day (Russell, 2023).

When enforcing your new rules, don't forget to communicate! Tell them, using words they'll understand, exactly what you're doing together and why. Summarize the main points here if needed, and then break things down like this:

- **Use age-appropriate language:** Tailor your communication to their developmental level. Use words and concepts they can understand and break down complex ideas into simpler terms.
- **Explain the purpose:** Clearly explain why certain rules are in place. Help them understand the reasons behind the rules by relating them to their well-being, safety, or the family's well-being.
- **Emphasize teamwork:** Frame rule enforcement as a collaborative effort. Let them know you're working together to create a happy and harmonious life for all involved. Make them feel part of the processes by encouraging them to participate and asking for their input if they can give it.

- **Provide concrete examples:** Use real-life scenarios and examples to illustrate the importance of following the rules. Help them understand the potential consequences of their actions and how their behavior affects them and others.
- **Use visual aids:** For ADHD children, visual aids facilitate information processing by simplifying abstract ideas into simple concepts (ADDRC, 2023). Use anything from flash cards and mnemonic devices for memory retention or gamified apps to keep them engaged and involved. Don't forget the simple power of paper and some coloring pencils! No, you don't have to be Van Gogh for this to work; just draw up a visual schedule that outlines the rules in action using pictures or symbols.

SETTING UP A DAILY ROUTINE

Now you know how and why to establish consistent boundaries and rules, let's look at what they look like in your day-to-day life. With predictability, they'll know what to expect and feel more secure and less anxious. With stability, they'll have a better chance of regulating their emotions, which reduces the likelihood of outbursts.

Morning Routine:

- **Wake up calmly:** Use a gentle alarm. Maybe it's a song they love.
- **Morning Hygiene:** Brush teeth and wash face. Keep the toothbrush in sight.
- **Get dressed:** Lay out clothes the night before to avoid decision fatigue.
- **Healthy breakfast:** Keep it simple and nutritious.
- **Prep time:** Check that their school bag is packed.
- **Quick activity:** A little stretching or a fun game to get the blood flowing.

After-School Routine:

- **Snack time:** They're probably hungry. Have some healthy snacks ready.
- **Downtime:** Let them unwind. Maybe 15 minutes of play before homework.
- **Check-in:** Ask about their day. Keep it light and engaging.

Homework Routine:

- **Designated spot:** Have a quiet, clutter-free area for homework.
- **Supplies ready:** Pencils, erasers, paper; have them all in one place.

- **Clear tasks:** Break homework into smaller chunks.
- **Time management:** Use a timer to work in short bursts and keep things fun.
- **Breaks:** Schedule a 5-minute break every 20 minutes.

Nighttime Routine:

- **Wind down:** Dim the lights and lower the noise an hour before bed.
- **Pajama time:** Changing into PJs signals it's almost bedtime.
- **Brush teeth:** Make it part of the routine, not a debate.
- **Storytime/chat:** This eases the transition to sleep.
- **Lights out:** Consistent bedtimes are non-negotiable!

This daily routine looks great on paper, doesn't it? But we all know things won't always go to plan with our little ADHD munchkin. Reality has a funny way of tossing plans out the window. So, expect the unexpected and be ready to adapt. ADHD might throw you a curveball, and that's okay; think of it as a chance to teach problem-solving and adaptability.

Tips for Setting up Your Routine:

When the routine goes sideways, take a deep breath, offer choices within boundaries, and gently steer back on track. If the morning routine gets hectic, maybe they choose their outfit the night before. Homework meltdown? Break it into chunks with fun breaks in between. Bedtime resistance? Introduce a calming activity they pick out. To make the activities in the routine stick, though, you should involve them in setting it up. This will make it more likely they'll stick to it while teaching them planning and organization skills.

- **Collaborate:** Sit down with them and map out the day together. Let them pick the color of their routine chart or the stickers when rewarding good behavior. This makes them feel in control and more invested.
- **Give them choices:** Offer them options within the routine to make them feel in control and keep them on track. For example, "Do you want to do your reading before or after your snack?"
- **Visual aids rock:** Use a whiteboard or a picture schedule; ADHD brains latch onto visuals. If they help draw or pick the images, even better. It's like gamifying the day.
- **Timing is everything:** Together, decide how long tasks should take. Set a timer they chose from the

store or download from the app store; they're a fun way to teach time management.

- **Make a big deal out of the small:** Did they stick to the morning routine? High-five! Small encouragements build confidence and positive associations with the routine.
- **Consistency counts:** Keep the big pillars of the day consistent, like mealtime, homework, and bedtime; it's the framework they rely on.
- **Review and revise:** At the end of the week, talk about what worked and what didn't. Maybe they found out they prefer doing homework at the kitchen table instead of their room; adjust as needed.

COMING UP

You've learned to listen, decode their needs, and respond without fueling the fire. It's like becoming a bilingual genius, where patience is your new second language. But let's be real; sometimes, despite your best efforts, emotions escalate, and behaviors spiral out of control. We take it all in stride. You've got tools now to weather those storms: consistent routines, clear expectations, and knowing when to bend without breaking. These are your shields against the outbursts and challenges. Now, as we wrap this chapter up, take a moment to acknowledge your progress; you're not just managing behaviors; you're teaching resilience and self-control.

Next up, we're creating your sanctuary, a stress-free home. Imagine a place where calm is king, and stress is a guest that never shows up. Get ready to transform your home into a distraction-free zone where everyone, especially your ADHD child, can thrive.

4

CREATING A STRESS-FREE HOME

My seven-year-old son Max has ADHD. Our living room used to look like a toy bomb exploded; Max couldn't focus, and tensions were high. Then, we got smart, ditched the clutter, and organized Max's toys into clear bins, labels, and all. After a while, Max knew where everything went, and the chaos started to settle a bit. We were really impressed with how this little change made such a big improvement. So, we went for some other calming techniques.

We cleared a corner of the room and dubbed it the "Quiet Zone." It's got a cozy bean bag, shelves with his favorite DVDs, and a stash of board games. We also made it device-free, and it became Max's go-to spot for unwinding. And guess what? The meltdowns dialed down, and focus dialed up. We realized after that a calm, organized space wasn't just nice to have; it made all the difference for Max's focus and our peace. Now, we're focusing on decluttering the rest of the house to reduce distraction everywhere!

STRATEGY 7: ESTABLISHING AN ADHD-FRIENDLY HOME ENVIRONMENT

When you're raising a child with ADHD, think of a structured home environment as the scaffolding that supports a building under construction. It's not just there; it's necessary. ADHD brains are buzzing with stimuli, and without a clear framework, it's like being in a constant fight with themselves, overwhelming and confusing. Structure translates to predictability, and predictability is like a steady beat in the noise of ADHD and daily life. It gives kids with ADHD a rhythm to move on. If, at home, things aren't as organized as they could be, everything feels up in the air; it's unsettling, like trying to walk through a busy street, blindfolded, without bumping into anyone. Now, picture a day when you know exactly what comes next. It's comforting, right? That's the power of routine for these children. When they know what to expect, their brains relax a bit, giving them an easier time to focus on keeping their emotions in check, doing chores, or just winding down for bed.

Consistency with routine is another cornerstone of an ADHD-friendly home. As we've already discussed, when kids with ADHD have consistent rules and consequences, they don't have to waste precious mental energy trying to figure out what's acceptable and what's not. All it takes is creating an environment where the ground rules are as clear as glass. Plus, when they know the lay of the land, they can handle it better, which translates to fewer meltdowns and more victories. Then there's the matter of independence. You might think that structure means hovering over your child's every move, but it's the opposite. A predictable home is a teaching ground for self-reliance. It's like training wheels on a bike; they're there for support, but they're still the ones pedaling. Let's not forget the emotional angle here. A structured home is a calm home, and calm is contagious. When kids with ADHD don't feel like they're living in a whirlwind, their stress levels drop. Lower stress means fewer mood swings and a happier, more harmonious household (Low, 2019). It's a win-win.

Organization and Decluttering Methods

By building that structured environment, you're not just keeping your child on track; you're giving them the tools to thrive. It's like crafting a personalized map for them to get around their world smoothly, and here's how to do exactly that. And no, you don't have to suddenly turn into a neat freak (if that's not already your forte); all you need to do is set up your home as a focus filter.

Step 1: Zone It Out

Carve out specific areas for specific activities. Homework happens at the desk, playtime in the corner with the toys, and eating at the dining table. With clear visual boundaries, they can switch between play and work mode without getting distracted.

Step 2: Simplify the Space

Too much stuff equals too many distractions. Keep only what's necessary in each zone. If it's homework time, only school supplies are on the desk. In this way, you're reducing the visual noise, and they can focus on what they need to do.

Step 3: Everything Has a Home

Assign a spot for everything; yes, everything. This way, they'll know exactly where to find their stuff and where to put it after they're done. Think of it as a reliable mental map for reducing brain overload.

Step 4: Label Like a Boss

Use labels liberally. When items have clear, readable labels, it's a no-brainer where things go. This is especially handy if their attention is a moving target. Clearly labeled items are like anchors that keep the focus from drifting.

Step 5: Use See-Through Containers

Out of sight, out of mind doesn't work well with ADHD. If they can see their stuff, they'll remember to use it and put it away. Plus, sifting through an unidentifiable box is a distraction minefield; clear bins equals problem solved.

Step 6: Color Code Like You Mean It

Colors grab attention and help in retaining information (Josel, 2022). So use this to your advantage with color-coded drawers, containers, towels, cables (one for each member of the family), and hangers so that they'll remember which clothes go where. Your child's brain will associate each color with its task, making it easier to stay on track. Get them involved, too; it'll be a fun team-building adventure for you both.

Step 7: The One-In-One-Out Rule

When a new toy or sweater comes in, an old one goes out. This keeps the clutter to a minimum, and decision-making becomes less overwhelming.

Step 8: Declutter Regularly

Schedule regular decluttering sessions. Make it a fun game to decide what stays and what goes. Less stuff means fewer distractions and smoother sailing through daily routines.

Step 9: Create a Distraction Box

When they get sidetracked by a non-related item, chuck it in the box. Out of sight, but not out of mind; they can get to it later, but, for now, it's not in the way.

Step 10: Maintain the Calm

Every evening, do a quick sweep together to reset the zones. Having this daily habit reinforces the structure and prepares the home for the next day's adventures.

Sensory-Friendly Methods

Sensory-friendly spaces aren't just nice-to-haves; they're an essential buffer zone from the sensory rush kids with ADHD face daily. Plus, they'll do the same for you, too! A room with soft hues, gentle lighting, and minimal fuss is like a visual sigh of relief for the ADHD brain, helping it to chill out and find its focus. It's not just about tranquility either. Sensory-friendly spaces help these kids feel secure because when their surroundings don't ambush them, they can process their thoughts and emotions better. You don't need to break the bank; just recognize that their needs are as unique as their talents and give them a space that acknowledges that. It's a big, comforting hug in the form of a room, and who doesn't need that?

- **Mute the palette:** Choose soothing, muted colors for walls and decor. Bright colors can overstimulate, so think pastels or earth tones that don't shout for attention (Sensory, 2023).
- **Soften the lights:** Harsh lighting flickers the nerves (Mae, 2021). Go for natural light with dimmable lamps and soft white bulbs. It keeps the vibe mellow, perfect for an ADHD brain already on high alert.
- **Introduce white noise:** White or brown noise quiets ADHD brains (Weinstein, 2022). Consistent, soft background sounds will mask jarring external noise, too. However, try it out first, as some children might become overstimulated.
- **Embrace the cozy:** For focus and attention issues, use soft fabrics and plush pillows. Weighted blankets are especially good for self-regulation and calming sensory issues (Drinks, 2019).
- **Be scent-sensitive:** Avoid strong fragrances and use unscented products or those with mild, natural scents to avoid aromatic overstimulation.
- **Silence the echo:** Hard surfaces bounce sound around. Carpets, rugs, and curtains absorb noise, making the space acoustically low-key.
- **Create a hideout:** Use a small tent or a canopy as a retreat spot when the world gets too much. It's a go-to safe zone for decompression.

- **Go natural:** The soft cascading sound of a water fountain or other water features evokes nature's vibe, which is naturally calming and helps with sensory regulation (Gold, 2023). Household plants, especially, have many benefits to our well-being: increased focus, attention, motivation, and decreased stress and impulsivity. Get the kids involved in taking care of them for an extra dopamine hit (Austin, 2023).
- **Balance sensory input:** Have a mix of sensory toys and calming tools available, like fidget spinners, stress balls, or weighted blankets, and use them whenever they're feeling overstimulated.

Creating this kind of space is about balance. You're crafting a sensory-friendly haven tailored to dial down the distractions and let an ADHD mind thrive. Now, let's look at how to keep your home in order. With work, kids, and other obligations, it's easy to get bogged down and leave household duties until later. If this sounds like you, then you'll need some easy and practical tips to keep things in check.

KEEPING ORDER AND CLEANLINESS

Even with an ADHD child turning every room into a potential hurricane zone, with the power of order, chaos doesn't stand a chance. When you've got systems in place, you're not just tidying up; you're building routines that stick. In terms of keeping things tidy, your home doesn't need to be like a spotless, magazine-cover home; as long as it doesn't trip up your child's focus with unexpected messes, you're good to go. Making their home supportive, where they won't be distracted by yesterday's craft project on the kitchen table, will help them thrive.

Ultimately, it's about more than just keeping a tidy house (although who doesn't want that!), but also giving your child ownership in their own space. It's a learning experience wrapped in the cloak of decluttering, where every picked-up toy and wiped-down counter is a step toward self-regulation.

But it's not just the ADHD brain that gets a boost from order. When your environment is sorted, your mind's to-do list shrinks. You're not mentally tripping over that pile of laundry or the stack of dishes. This decluttered space lowers the background stress for everyone, dialing down the family anxiety meter. This is because mental health and tidying up are connected (Gordon, 2023). Just like unwanted background sound, visual clutter bombards our senses, interfering with our ability to process information. When you clear away the mess, you're essentially turning down the visual noise. This decluttering lets the brain relax and focus better because fewer stimuli are competing for attention (Alton, 2017). A tidy space encourages well-being and accomplishment, giving everyone in the household a mental breather. It's like each neatly arranged shelf and organized room tells your brain, "Hey, it's okay to chill out now."

The following practical tips and systems for keeping order don't just lighten the cognitive load for the ADHD mind; they create a more peaceful environment for everyone by reducing stress and making it easier to concentrate for the whole crew:

- **Daily declutter sessions:** Set a timer for 10 minutes each day. Blitz through a room, scooping up misplaced items. You're not deep-cleaning; just keep the chaos at bay.
- **Everything has a home:** Assign every item a spot. Label bins if you have to. It's easier to put things back when they've got a dedicated nook.
- **The four-box method:** Get your hand on four hefty boxes and label them: Trash, Donate, Keep, and Decide later. This will help you avoid making tough decisions when it comes to decluttering, as your goals are clearly defined within the model of the boxes.
- **Clean as you go:** Just finished eating? Wipe down the table right then. Finished with the toothpaste? Back in the cabinet, it goes. Small actions: big impact.
- **The five-minute rule:** If it takes less than five minutes, do it immediately. Hang up your coat, answer that email, or make your bed.

- **Weekly purge day:** Choose a day each week for a mini purge. Check a drawer, a shelf, or a closet, and keep it simple but consistent.
- **Vertical space is your friend:** Use walls to keep floors clear and install shelves, over-the-door storage, or pegboards.
- **The basket system:** Each family member gets a basket, and throughout the day, any stray items belonging to them go in there. At the end of the day, they empty it and put things back where they came from.
- **Nightly reset:** Before bed, do a quick sweep to reset common areas. Mornings feel better without yesterday's clutter looming over you.

Having learned about establishing an ADHD-friendly home environment, let's explore another essential component: family nutrition and self-care. Nothing too demanding, just creating an environment that complements your ADHD-friendly strategies, promoting well-being and optimal functioning for you and your child.

STRATEGY 8: FAMILY NUTRITION AND SELF-CARE

While nutrition alone may not be a cure for ADHD, it can certainly make a difference in managing symptoms and improving your child's behavior. All it takes is making mindful choices about the foods to offer, and you'll give your child essential nutrients that support brain health and perhaps even alleviate some of their symptoms.

Certain nutrients, such as omega-3 fatty acids, zinc, iron, and magnesium, are essential for brain development. When these nutrients are lacking, it can affect neurotransmitter production and regulation in the brain, contributing to ADHD symptoms in some, but not all, children with nutrient deficiencies. Studies have also shown that a diet high in refined sugars, artificial additives, and processed foods can make ADHD symptoms worse (Nurseline, 2023). These foods spike blood sugar levels, leading to energy crashes and concentration issues. There are also some food additives, like artificial colors and preservatives, that may exacerbate hyperactivity symptoms (NHS, 2017).

On the flip side, a nutrient-rich diet can reduce ADHD symptoms (Roybal et al., 2023). Foods rich in omega-3 fatty acids, such as fatty fish, chia seeds, and walnuts, have been shown to improve cognitive ability. Including whole grains, fruits, vegetables, lean proteins, and healthy fats in your child's diet can also support their overall health and brain function (Editors, 2022b).

So, what does this look like in terms of a menu?

Creating Balanced, Nutritious Meal Plans

For creating balanced and nutritious meal plans for your family, including your ADHD child, there are some fundamentals to keep in mind:

- **Focus on whole foods rich in nutrients:** Pack plenty of fruits, vegetables, whole grains, lean proteins, and healthy fats into your meals. These foods have essential vitamins, minerals, and antioxidants that go a long way in boosting mood, cardiovascular health, and other benefits to support a healthy brain and body (Crichton-Stuart, 2020).
- **Aim for a good balance of macronutrients in each meal:** Include a source of protein, like chicken, fish, tofu, or beans, to help stabilize blood sugar levels and keep you energized throughout the day. Pair it with complex carbohydrates like whole grains, sweet potatoes, or quinoa for a steady release of energy. Don't forget to include healthy fats like avocados, nuts, and olive oil, as they are great for brain health and nutrient absorption (Schewitz, 2023).
- **Pay attention to the micronutrients:** Eat colorful fruits and vegetables, as they are packed with vitamins, minerals, and antioxidants that support

cognitive function. For example, greens like broccoli, spinach, or kale are rich in folate, a nutrient linked to brain health (Harvard, 2021).

- **Minimize processed foods:** Sugary snacks and artificial additives can disrupt blood sugar levels and interfere with an already unregulated ADHD brain (Drake, 2023). Instead, choose homemade meals and snacks you can control and prepare using wholesome ingredients.

By following a curated meal plan full of balanced, nutritious meals, you not only support your child's well-being and manage their symptoms but also make sure they eat the right foods that enhance their cognitive function. To further optimize their nutrition, let's look at some specific foods to eat and avoid with ADHD, the impact of which can be significant on their attention span, behavior, and brain health.

Foods and Ingredients to Eat With ADHD:

1. Fatty fish (salmon, sardines).
2. Nuts and seeds (walnuts, chia seeds).
3. Fresh fruits (blueberries, oranges).
4. Leafy greens (spinach, kale).
5. Whole grains (quinoa, brown rice).
6. Lean proteins (chicken, turkey).
7. Legumes (beans, lentils).
8. Eggs.

9. Greek yogurt.
10. Avocado.

Foods and Ingredients to Avoid With ADHD:

1. Processed foods (chips, cookies).
2. Sugary snacks and beverages (sodas, candies).
3. Artificial additives and preservatives (artificial colors, MSG).
4. Refined carbohydrates (white bread, white rice).
5. Dairy products (milk, cheese).
6. Gluten-containing foods (wheat, barley).
7. Artificial sweeteners (aspartame, sucralose).
8. High-fructose corn syrup.
9. Caffeinated drinks (coffee, energy drinks).
10. Fast food meals.

This list is a general guideline; kids are fussy and might also have sensitivities when it comes to certain foods. By all means, feel free to consult with a healthcare professional or registered dietitian for personalized recommendations. They'll work with you to put a personalized plan together based on your child's dietary needs and preferences.

Get the Family Involved

Getting everyone in the family on board with meal prep does wonders. You dodge the sibling rivalry bullet right away; no one's feeling left out because they're all in on the action. It's about making every kid feel like a VIP, part of a team where their ADHD sibling isn't hogging the limelight. They chop, stir, and learn together, which squashes any brewing jealousy. Plus, it's not just about avoiding the green-eyed monster; it's a bonding buffet! They're laughing, measuring out ingredients, and maybe even learning a thing or two about healthy eating. They're not just making meals; they're making memories. And your ADHD child? They're soaking up skills and confidence like a sponge, with their siblings right there cheering them on. It's a win-win: No one is on the sidelines, and everyone's dishing out love and support. Here are some tips to kick things off:

- Assign age-appropriate tasks to each family member, like peeling veggies for the little ones and chopping for the older kids, so everyone's got their own job.
- Rotate roles regularly and let each person take turns being the "head chef" to keep things fresh and give everyone a taste of responsibility.
- Plan meals together and decide on the week's menu as a crew.
- Create a family recipe book; encourage everyone to add their recipes or tweak existing ones to make them their own.
- Celebrate cultural heritage or explore new cuisines together.

- Have a quick family meeting post-meal to chat about what rocked and what could be tweaked.
- Remember to high-five all around for jobs well done. There's nothing like a bit of cheerleading to keep spirits high.

SELF-CARE ROUTINES

After getting the nutrition down, now on to self-care. Self-care isn't just a buzzword; it's the glue holding the chaos at bay, especially in a home bustling with ADHD energy. Think of it as your family's mental health work-out. For parents, it's your oxygen mask; you know how flight attendants say to put yours on first before helping others? That's self-care; it keeps you sane, grounded, and ready to handle whatever cereal spill or homework melt-down comes next.

For kids, it's equally vital. ADHD or not, they're juggling school, friends, hormones; it's a lot. Self-care routines help them feel in control, a moment to breathe in a world that's always buzzing. They get to regroup, recharge, and jump back into it refreshed.

Together, when you commit to self-care, you're building a stress-resistant fortress. You're teaching your kids to value their well-being, and that's a life lesson more precious than gold. Showing them that in the rush of life, finding a quiet moment to be is not just important; it's a necessity. Here are some relaxation techniques and activities that promote mental and physical well-being:

- Kick off with a family dance to get those endorphins pumping. Crank up the volume and let loose in the living room. It's a workout, a laugh, and a surefire stress buster all rolled into one (Strauss, 2020).
- Pair up together or as a group for some yoga. Try out partner poses to build balance and trust, all while stretching away the day's tension.
- Get artsy, whether it's coloring, painting, or sculpting playdough; it gives people an outlet to express themselves and calm their minds (Loeuy, 2022).
- Go on nature walks or treasure hunts. Mother Nature's fresh air plus a bit of adventure equals a clear head and a happy heart (Mind, 2021).
- Set up a mini-challenge, like who can build the tallest Lego tower. It's a playful competition that also sharpens focus and fine motor skills (Wellness Centre, 2019).

It's not just about physical health; mental and emotional well-being is equally important. So, carve out quiet time for reading or listening to music. These moments of calm can be a relief for the ADHD brain's constant buzz.

- Mix in some mindfulness or breathing exercises. They're like a remote control for the brain, helping to fast-forward through stress or pause before a meltdown.
- Keep a gratitude jar. Everyone drops in notes about what they're thankful for. It's a visual reminder of the good stuff, keeping spirits high and hearts grateful.

COMING UP

You've been rocking it, turning your home into an ADHD-friendly zone that's more a zen garden than a wild jungle. It's calm, structured, and nutrition-heavy, setting the stage for everyone's emotional well-being to blossom. But we need to take it to another level. In the next chapter, we're exploring emotional regulation and coping skills. These are key skills for handling whatever ADHD life throws your way. The strategies you've learned here? They're the roots that will support the growth of these advanced skills in Chapter 5. Get ready to plant the seeds to build some emotional muscle!

5

FOSTERING EMOTIONAL REGULATION AND COPING SKILLS

Your child can't lead you into their chaos. You must lead them out of theirs.

— DR. SIGGIE

STRATEGY 9: TEACHING SELF-REGULATION TECHNIQUES

Self-regulation is like the brain's thermostat; it's how you adjust your feelings to match the situation. An ADHD child's thermostat is often a bit unstable. They might feel the heat more quickly like going from zero to a hundred when they're losing at their favorite game, or a small setback feels like an iceberg hit:

- A friend says something that rubs them the wrong way, and boom, it's tears or tantrums.
- You tell them no at the sweet aisle, and there are screams all the way back to the car.
- With homework, one tricky math problem can crank their frustration from a two to a ten.
- A playground mishap causes a meltdown because their emotional control is still learning the ropes.

They're not being like this on purpose, overreacting like it's the end of the world; they're just working with a different set of tools. It's tough because while their buddies develop emotional breaks earlier, ADHD kids are often left behind (Buzanko, 2023). This goes beyond feeling things more intensely; it has to do with struggling to put those feelings on hold so they can respond, not just react. And that's the race we're running, helping them build better coping skills so you can guide them toward better emotional control and better day-to-day living.

Read Together

Step 1: Pick a book, either a paperback, E-book, or even audiobook, something with fun characters and a plot thick with feelings.

Step 2: Get cozy. Plop down in a comfy nook and grab some snacks—let's make this fun.

Step 3: Read together; you read a page, then let them (if they can) read the next.

Step 4: As you read, pause when a character feels something and ask, "How do you think they feel?" Connect it to a feeling they know and let them describe the frustration or anger, putting words to emotions they know all too well.

Step 5: Identify any triggers that come up by talking about what made the character feel that way. "See, the toy breaking made them mad. What things make you feel mad?"

Step 6: When you hit a part where a character blows their top, talk about the consequences. Discuss alternative reactions and the different outcomes they might lead to.

Step 7: Explore some calming solutions when the character calms down; talk about it, "They took deep breaths to calm down. What can we do when we're mad?" Brainstorm ideas together and show them there are tools to deal with frustration or overwhelming emotions.

Step 8: Practice together by simulating the emotion-regulation strategy. Pretend you're both angry, then breathe deeply or count to 10.

Step 9: Praise and Encourage: After the exercise, praise and encourage them for their effort. "You did a great job understanding the character's feelings!"

Step 10: Apply these techniques in real life the next time they get overwhelmed. Gently remind them of the story. "Remember how they calmed down? Let's try that," or "Remember what they could've done differently?" It's a nudge towards using those emotional tools in their own world.

Storytelling

Start by grabbing a comfy spot and some colorful drawing supplies. Tell your child they're going to create their very own *Emotion Adventure Book*. Each page represents a different emotion.

Step 1: Pick an Emotion

Ask them, "What feeling shall we explore first?" Say they choose "happiness."

Step 2: Draw and Personalize

Draw a character feeling happy; maybe it's a grinning frog. Ask, "What makes Mr. Frog so cheerful?" They might say, "He's playing with friends."

Step 3: Identify Triggers

Discuss what triggers this emotion. "When do you feel like Mr. Frog?"

Step 4: Create a Story

Now, create a little story. "Once, Mr. Frog felt left out, so he asked to join the game. How do you think that made him feel?"

Step 5: Problem-Solve

If the emotion is harsh, like anger, brainstorm solutions together. "What could Mr. Frog do when he's mad?"

Step 6: Reflect

After drawing and storytelling, reflect on the day. "Did you feel like Mr. Frog at any point today?"

Exercise and Physical Movement

Regular physical activity has profound positive effects in helping children with ADHD refocus their attention and regulate their emotions. Exercise or physical activity increases blood flow and oxygen to the brain. This, in turn, stimulates the release of neurotransmitters like dopamine, norepinephrine, and serotonin, which are essential for regulating attention, mood, and emotions (Lahoti, 2023). These neurotransmitters help to improve focus, reduce impulsivity, and enhance overall cognitive function. So, when you see your child running around or playing sports, know that their brain is getting a workout, too, and it's helping them feel and do their best!

There are more amazing benefits, too. Studies have consistently shown that exercise can improve attention and concentration in children with ADHD. For example, a study published in the National Library of Medicine reported that just 20 minutes of moderate to intense aerobic exercise markedly improved attention and reduced symptoms of ADHD symptoms (Mehren et al., 2020). Another study published in the Biomedical Journal demonstrated that regular physical activity improved cognitive performance and reduced hyperactivity and impulsivity in children with ADHD (Chan et al., 2021). Another win-win for their well-being is that exercise has also been found to have a positive impact on emotional regulation in children with ADHD. Plus, physical activity releases feel-good chemicals in the brain, helping to reduce stress, anxiety, and frustration. It's like a natural mood booster! Regular exercise also provides a healthy outlet for excessive energy, allowing children to release tension and improve their emotional well-being. So, encourage regular exercise to help them focus better, feel happier, and manage their emotions better. Think of activities like outdoor play, sports, dance, yoga, or even simple exercises like jumping jacks or running in place. The key is to find something they'll enjoy and can do regularly.

- **Outdoor play as an outlet for their energy and improve focus (Lucchetti, 2023):**

  - Running, jumping, climbing, and playing catch outside.
  - Join them in a game of tag or create an obstacle course together.

- **Sports to promote discipline, cooperation, and focus (Health Direct, 2018):**

  - Enroll them in team sports like soccer, basketball, or swimming.
  - Cheer them on during their games to make it a positive experience.

- **Yoga to improve concentration and reduce stress (Turis, 2021):**

  - Yoga combines physical movement with mindfulness.
  - Find kid-friendly yoga videos or attend a local yoga class together.

- **Dance to express emotions and improve inhibition (Tao et al., 2022):**

  - Encourage them to dance to their favorite music.
  - Create a dance routine together or have a dance party at home.

- **Martial Arts to learn self-discipline, self-control, and focus (Boring, 2022):**

  - Think classes like karate or taekwondo.
  - Find a martial arts studio that offers classes for children

- **Biking or rollerblading to improve focus and coordination (Clifton, 2021):**

  - Go for a bike ride or rollerblade together.
  - Explore local parks or bike trails for a change of scenery.

- **Mindful walking to promote attentiveness and grounding (Sutton, 2020):**

  - Take them outside in nature, and go on mindful walks where you focus on the present moment.
  - Encourage them to notice their surroundings, listen to the sounds, and feel the sensations in their body as they walk.

Tips for Getting Them Involved:

- Make it fun and engaging by turning exercises into games or challenges.
- Set aside dedicated time for physical activity each day.
- Provide positive reinforcement and praise them even just for trying.
- Join in the activities with your child to make it a bonding experience.
- Be patient and understanding if they struggle initially. Focus on progress, not perfection. For example, you can say, "Let's go to the park and play a game of tag. I'll chase you, and you can try to run and dodge me. It'll be so much fun!"

Finding activities they'll enjoy and adding them to their routine will make it more likely for them to get involved willingly. So, get creative, and have fun!

Recognizing and Responding to Their Feelings

Let's add one more self-regulation technique to your arsenal with emotional recognition and response. When kids with ADHD can identify their emotions, they'll learn how to communicate them, which means improved social skills and a stronger sense of self-awareness because their self-esteem and confidence will grow. Children who understand how to respond to their emotions are also learning life skills. They'll learn healthy ways to cope with stress, regulate their behavior, and make better decisions. It's like giving them a toolbox filled with strategies for success!

Step 1: Teach Emotional Vocabulary

- Help them develop their emotional vocabulary by introducing emotions and their corresponding feelings.
- Use flashcards to illustrate different emotions.
- Discuss examples of situations that might elicit these emotions.

Step 2: Recognize Physical and Behavioral Cues

- Guide them in recognizing physical and behavioral cues associated with different emotions.

- For example, when they feel angry, they might clench their fists or have an increased heart rate. When they feel sad, they might have tears in their eyes or withdraw socially.

Step 3: Practice Emotional Check-Ins

- Encourage them to regularly check in with their emotions throughout the day.
- They can do this through verbal prompts or a feelings chart.
- Ask them how they're feeling and help them label their emotions for better self-awareness.

Step 4: Develop Coping Strategies

- Provide them with coping strategies that will help them manage their emotions.
- Teach them techniques like taking a time out, deep breathing, or other calming activities.
- Let them choose what to use as a calming technique. This way they'll likely use it.

Step 5: Validate and Encourage Expression

- When they express their emotions, validate their feelings and provide a safe space for them to express themselves.
- Avoid dismissing or belittling their emotions.

- Encourage them to use their words to express how they feel.

Step 6: Reflect and Learn

- After an outburst, meltdown, tantrum, or other emotional reaction, reflect with your child on how they handled the situation.
- Discuss what worked well and what could be improved; this is a great way to promote growth and self-reflection.

Now that we've explored self-regulation techniques, let's move on to techniques for calming and de-escalation. These strategies are interconnected because when kids learn to recognize and regulate their emotions, they're able to deal with challenging situations and use strategies for calming themselves down.

STRATEGY 10: TECHNIQUES FOR CALMING AND DE-ESCALATION

Calming techniques for kids with ADHD are like secret weapons for managing those big, explosive emotions. Consider a little one, Daryl, who's got ADHD. Picture him in a classroom where it's all too noisy, and suddenly, he's having a meltdown. But because Daryl's parents have been helping to practice some calming techniques, he realizes he's about to lose his cool and instead finds a quiet corner to breathe deeply and count to ten. He's got his very own set of emotional tools at his disposal. Parents play a huge role here; they're like the coaches teaching young minds how to use these tools. Take Anne, another kid with ADHD; she used to throw a fit every time homework got frustrating. Her parents stepped in, helped her recognize when she was getting agitated, and Voilà; now she takes a five-minute doodling break to reset.

What's awesome is that these techniques are more than just quick fixes; they're building blocks for better emotional control in the long term. Let's not forget how this spills over into daily life; kids who get the hang of these techniques tend to do better at school, too (Graziano et al., 2007). They'll also get better at making friends, and yes, they give their parents a bit of peace, too.

Mindfulness

Step 1: Catch the Signs

Notice when their mood starts shifting; maybe their face scrunches up, or they get fidgety. That's your cue.

Step 2: Pause Everything

Stop what you're doing and tell them, "Let's take a quick pause."

Step 3: Deep Breathing

Guide them to take deep breaths, say, "Breathe in like you're smelling a flower, and out like you're blowing out a candle."

Step 4: Engage Their Senses

Ask them to describe what they see, hear, or feel. For example, "Can you hear the clock ticking? What does the chair feel like under your hands?"

Step 5: Naming Emotions

Help them put a name to their feelings. "Are you feeling frustrated/overwhelmed/sad? That's totally okay."

Step 6: Offer Choices

Give them options for what to do next, "Do you want to draw or squeeze a stress ball?"

Step 7: Reflect Together

After they've calmed down, talk about it. "How did that deep breathing feel?"

With each step, you're teaching them to recognize their emotions, pause before reacting, and handle difficult feelings like a pro. They'll start to realize they're in charge of their own chill-out time, which is pretty empowering for a kid with ADHD. Plus, they'll carry these skills everywhere, from the playground to the classroom.

Controlled Breathing

This exercise is designed to help children manage their emotions, particularly when they're on the verge of a tantrum or meltdown. When using it with them, call it "dragon breathing" to make it more appealing and fun.

Step 1: Find a quiet place where you both can sit and won't be disturbed.

Step 2: Ask them to take a deep breath through their nose, like they're smelling a giant, colorful flower. They'll need to take in a long, slow breath for relaxation.

Step 3: Ask them to hold their breath for a short count of three to make them aware of their breathing and allow them to pause for a few moments.

Step 4: After a few beats, ask them to breathe out with a long and slow exhale through the mouth, with the child imagining they're cooling down a hot drink. It's at this point the release of tension happens and will soothe the nerves.

Step 5: Encourage them to repeat this breathing cycle five times. The repetition helps cement the practice while reshaping their emotional state, steering them away from a meltdown, and guiding them to a calmer state of mind.

Quiet Activities to Calm Down

Each of these activities switches up the vibe and gently nudges them from frenzied to calm. Give them a try and find out which one your little one resonates with the most.

- **Puzzle time:** Slide a jigsaw puzzle in front of them and ask them, "Hey, let's see how many pieces you can fit in five minutes." It's a sneaky way to shift focus and get those fine motor skills working.
- **Coloring central:** Whip out a coloring book and some crayons, and say, "Pick three colors for this picture." It's low-key and keeps their hands and minds busy.
- **Play-Doh party:** Hand them some Play-Doh and challenge them with, "Can you make a snake or a burger?"
- **Reading retreat:** Grab a picture book and plop down next to them. Go with, "Help me count all the red things on this page."
- **Whisper game:** Start whispering, and they'll have to quiet down to hear you. It's like, "I'm going to tell you a secret story, but you need to be super quiet."

Sensory and Fidget Toys

These toys give kids a physical way to channel their feelings, no matter what they are. Plus, they help with self-regulation. Think of them as pressure valves for your child's emotional steam. When they start bubbling up with feelings, hand them a fidget toy. It's something about the repetitive motion—twisting, squishing, spinning—that flips the switch in their brain from "Ahhh!" to "Ahh..." It's the tactile input that does the trick, giving them something to focus on, which can dial down the intensity of their emotions.

Now, for the arsenal. Here's a list of some sensory and fidget toys you might want to stash for a rainy day:

- Fidget spinners
- Stress balls
- Sensory Rings
- Fidget Cubes
- Kinetic sand
- Squishies
- Tangle toys
- Slime
- Weighted stuffed animals
- Chewelry (jewelry that's safe to chew on)

Limiting Electronic Use and Screen Time

Limiting electronic use and screen time for children is like trying to pry a treasure map out of their hands; it's their gateway to endless entertainment, and they'll guard it with all their might! But it has several benefits.

Excessive screen time can actually make ADHD symptoms worse, cause sleep problems, and, according to 85% of caregivers, impact behavior as well. (McQueen, 2022). This isn't to say that screen time contributes to ADHD; it just sucks away precious time that could be spent on other things that promote calm and cognitive function. Setting boundaries, then, offers them the opportunity for self-regulation and relaxation activities. Spending less time in front of screens also encourages physical activity and social interaction (Muppalla et al., 2023), both of which are essential for an ADHD child's development.

This is advice only, so don't feel guilty if you reach for your phone or iPad when a meltdown is on the horizon; sometimes, it's the only thing that helps at the moment. As long as you're making an effort to set boundaries and manage screen time in a balanced way, you're doing your best to support your child's well-being. Embrace the fact that technology can provide temporary relief and a much-needed distraction, giving you and your child a chance to regroup and find calm when things get too much. In the meantime, consider giving them a certain number of hours per day. In general, researchers recommend one to two hours of screen time per day for children and less than one hour for children between two and five (Smith, 2023). But you can monitor and adjust this as you see fit and find some alternative activities to replace a few hours of technology a week:

- **Set clear boundaries:** You say, "Hey, 30 minutes of tablet time, and then it's off." Stick to it and use a timer to make it official; no arguments when the beep goes off.
- **Get them moving:** Physical activity is gold for burning that extra energy. Try a "freeze dance" game. Music goes on; they go wild; the music stops, and they freeze. It's fun and tires them out.
- **Creative time:** Crafting isn't just for making a mess; it's hands-on and takes some concentration. Maybe they're into drawing, painting, or sculpting with clay. Let them express themselves.
- **Nature's a biggie:** Get outdoors; a trip to the park, a hike in the woods, or just chilling in the backyard can reset their mood.

Counseling or Therapy Options

No matter how hard you try, sometimes there's just no getting past the fact that their meltdowns are more epic than an erupting volcano. When nothing you do seems to help, it's time to get a professional involved.

Counseling or therapy is your go-to when you're scratching your head, wondering why time-outs and talks aren't cutting it. ADHD brains are wired differently; they need different strategies. Therapists are like emotional electricians; they know the wiring and can teach your child how to flick the right switches. If you're considering this route and feeling ashamed or like you've failed? Stop that right now. Asking for help means you're all-in on parenting; you're not giving up; you're leveling up and giving them the best shot at handling their emotions confidently.

Therapy isn't just for your child either; it's for you, too. You'll learn how to support your little one and maybe even pick up a few tips for yourself. It's a team effort, and therapy is your best friend for building those emotion-management muscles.

- Cognitive-behavioral therapy (CBT) is a solid pick. Therapists work with kids to recognize their thought patterns, break down overwhelming emotions, and give them strategies to handle them, like problem-solving or facing fears bit by bit.
- Another great option is Play Therapy, especially for the younger crowd. It's not just playtime; it's strategic. Through play, kids express what's bothering them and learn to deal with it without even realizing they're in therapy.

- Then there's Family Therapy; this one's a team effort. It involves the whole family in understanding what your child's going through and how you can all work together for a smoother ride at home.
- For social butterflies or kids who might feel they're the only ones struggling, Group Therapy can be a hit. They get to meet others in the same boat, share experiences, and pick up new coping skills.
- Mindfulness-Based Interventions (MBI) programs can also help kids get a grip on their emotions by focusing on the here and now rather than letting overwhelming emotions take the wheel.

Therapy isn't just there to help you both calm down a tantrum; it's to help build skills for life. If your child learns these skills now, they're set with better ways to tackle the ups and downs that come their way.

COMING UP

Teaching yourself, and your child, emotional regulation and coping skills means you're setting them up for better control of their feelings and behavior in everyday life. But you're also laying the foundation for their academic success. When kids can manage their emotions, they're more likely to stay focused, participate in class, and handle the demands of school. Let's now look at how you can support their academic performance.

6

SUPPORTING ACADEMIC SUCCESS

ADHD school students can benefit from both interventions and accommodations. A *Journal of School Psychology* study (Harrison et al., 2020) spotlights the difference between interventions (skills students learn, parent-teacher collaboration, and better study habits) and accommodations (tweaking the environment or tasks to help students cope). The study focuses on common ADHD challenges in middle school students, like multi-tasking, following spoken instructions, and staying focused. The kids who get targeted interventions like teaching organization, note-taking, and self-management do better than those with only accommodations.

The bottom line: Teaching practical skills for coping in schools and advocating for accommodations can really help ADHD students shine. It's a solid nod to parents and schools to consider beefing up their strategies for students with ADHD. The best part is you can learn exactly how to do this for yourself!

STRATEGY 11: COLLABORATING WITH EDUCATORS FOR ACCOMMODATIONS

Your child is smart and creative, but sometimes they struggle to keep up in class, stay focused, or manage their impulses. Now, think about the powerhouse team that could be formed if you, as a parent, join forces with educators.

ADHD can manifest in several different ways, and what works for one child might not work for another. That's why parents and teachers need to be on the same wavelength. When they communicate regularly, they can swap notes on what's happening at school and home. Then, teachers can offer insights into academic and social behaviors, while parents can share strategies that work at home. It's like creating a joint home and school personalized system for supporting them. Without this communication, how will a teacher know what your child needs help with if you don't tell them? Or how can you reinforce positive behaviors at home if you're in the dark about what's happening in the classroom?

Communication with teachers also builds trust and understanding. Imagine how supported and validated your child will feel if they see their parents and teachers working together. This collaboration will boost their confidence and motivation (WGU, 2021), which, let's be honest, is half the battle with ADHD.

Open communication does more than address challenges; it celebrates progress, no matter how small. Every step forward deserves a pat on the back, and when everyone's sharing the successes, it creates an environment of positivity that's infectious. So, let's break down those walls, keep the lines open, and watch as this partnership transforms the ADHD challenge into a path of opportunities.

Advocating for Accommodations in the Classroom

The first step in this is advocating for ADHD accommodations. If you don't know already, these tweaks and tools level the playing field for students with ADHD. Things like seating them where they're least likely to get distracted, maybe up front by the teacher or away from windows with a distractive view. Then, there's the time factor. Extended time on tests isn't a matter of taking it easy; they're there to allow students to show what they know without the timer of a pressure cooker ticking in their heads. Accommodations also help with how things are done. Things like getting instructions one step at a time can mean the difference between understanding and wondering, *What did I miss?* Plus, having a set of class notes ready can be a lifesaver when focus wanes. No matter what your child needs to do better in the classroom, the main thing is creating an environment where they're able to grow academically and socially.

In advocating for accommodations in the classroom, most countries are covered under federal law, which recognizes ADHD as a disability, guaranteeing students with ADHD receive the necessary support to succeed in their educational environment. In the United States, for instance, two key laws come into play: The Individuals with Disabilities Education Act (IDEA) and Section 504 of the Rehabilitation Act (Department of Education, 2016).

IDEA provides specialized education and Individualized Education Programs (IEPs) for students who qualify, while Section 504 covers any child with a disability that substantially limits one or more major life activities, including learning. Under these laws, you have the right to request an evaluation for your child at no cost to you.

Knowing your rights and the laws that protect your child helps you work with educators to create an effective, tailored plan, and you can request, in writing, an evaluation from the school. Once your child is eligible, you'll need to decide between an IEP (Individualized Education Program) or a 504 plan. In terms of strategy, keep everything documented, every meeting, call, letter, or email with the school. Be clear about your child's needs, but also listen. The goal here is collaboration, not confrontation.

Here's a quick list of accommodations you might consider:

- **Seating arrangements:** Ask for a seat away from distractions and closer to the teacher.
- **Breaks:** Frequent short breaks can help your child recharge.
- **Extended time:** More time on tests and assignments can ease the pressure.
- **Alternate test formats:** Oral exams or fill-in-the-blanks might work better than multiple-choice.
- **Instructions:** Giving instructions one step at a time can keep things manageable.
- **Note-taking assistance:** Maybe a buddy system or teacher-provided notes.
- **Homework adjustments:** Possibly fewer problems or assignments broken into chunks.
- **Fidget aids:** Something small to fidget with can help with focus.
- **Behavioral plan:** Positive reinforcement strategies that reward good behavior.
- **Communication plan:** Regular check-ins between teachers and parents.

You're the expert on your child. Stick to your guns, but also be ready to adapt because what works when they're young may change as they get older. Stay in touch with the teachers and tweak the plan as you go.

The Benefits of Individualized Education Programs (IEPs) and 504 Plans

The big difference between the two? An IEP is a beefier plan under the Individuals with Disabilities Education Act (IDEA), offering more services and protections (Kessler, 2023), while a 504 is under the Rehabilitation Act, focusing on accommodations in the standard learning environment (Low, 2022). Both aim to support your child, but the route they take to get there varies, as does the help they offer.

- IEPs fit students with more intensive special education needs. They're detailed and legally binding, laying out specific educational goals, the services to be provided, and how progress gets measured. It also covers social and behavioral skills and even life beyond the classroom. They'll help kids with speech needs as well as occupational therapy. It's comprehensive, and because it's legally binding, schools have got to follow through.
- A 504 Plan is flexible and provides the tools your child needs to access learning on the same level as their peers. This plan evens the playing field, providing accommodations like extra test time or a quiet room for work. It's for kids who can learn within a general education curriculum but just need a few adjustments to manage their ADHD.

The goal is less about specialized services and more about giving your child the chance to make the most of their education.

Both plans are a pretty big deal for you and your child. An IEP transforms a school experience with its personalized approach, while a 504 Plan removes barriers to learning. Either way, your child gets a fair shot academically, and that's what really counts.

Once you're on the know-how about teaming up with teachers to tailor your child's learning environment, it's time to bring that same spirit of customization home. Just as an IEP or 504 Plan individualizes school support, setting up productive study habits at home will make them more confident about managing their ADHD and academic responsibilities.

STRATEGY 12: ESTABLISHING EFFECTIVE STUDY HABITS

We've already covered how routine is like your child's safety net. When thoughts, tasks, or distractions disrupt the ADHD brain, structured and consistent study routines will help keep things on track. Routines bring predictability in an unpredictable ADHD world. When kids know what's coming, it reduces anxiety, so they're not on edge, wondering what the next study session throws at them. Instead, they've got a blueprint, a comfy groove that their brain starts to recognize and settle into.

Knowing what to do and when doesn't just mean knowing when to hit the books; it's also about how. Structured routines can mean starting with the toughest subject or using a timer to break the work into manageable sections. This kind of consistency turns confusion into focus. Over time, these routines become second nature, and that's when the magic happens. Kids start to manage their time, take the initiative, and, most importantly, learn how to learn. Here's how to bring effective study habits into their routine:

- Kick things off by setting a regular study time; this signals the brain that it's go-time for learning.
- Break tasks into small, achievable goals so your child can taste success and stay motivated.
- Use visual timers to manage focus periods, followed by short, active breaks to burn off that extra energy.
- Checklists are a great way for them to tick off completed tasks; it's satisfying and keeps track of progress.
- Consistent praise for sticking to the routine does wonders, too.
- Mix up the subjects to keep boredom at bay, and always wrap up with a quick review to reinforce the day's learning.

Keeping It Distraction-Free:

- Start by carving out a study spot as quiet as a mouse; think of it as a no-go zone for distractions. Make sure this space is used for study time only so your child's brain knows it's game time when they sit down.
- Keep it clutter-free; a tidy desk equals a focused mind.
- Now, tech is tricky; it's a helper, and a focus hijacker rolled into one. So, keep gadgets that aren't study buddies out of arm's reach during homework hours.
- Use noise-canceling headphones if the house can't go into library mode, or try some gentle white noise to drown out the background buzz.
- Lighting is important, too; a well-lit room keeps sleep away and the focus sharp.
- Have all the necessary supplies on hand—pencils sharpened, paper ready—to avoid any "I gotta get…" interruptions.

Study Techniques

Study techniques provide a framework that transforms jumbled thoughts into organized action. With the right strategies, children with ADHD can manage their time, stay on task, and actually retain what they learn (Jacobson, 2023). Techniques like chunking material or using mnemonic devices make learning stick, not just for the test tomorrow, but for the long haul. Plus, when these kids see that they can conquer their study sessions, they're more likely to take on new challenges. Attributing their efforts to their achievements breeds motivation and a positive attitude toward learning (Borba, 2022).

The Pomodoro Technique

Like interval training but for studying: The frequent breaks with the Pomodoro technique keep stress in check and help maintain a high level of concentration during focus time. Plus, as these cycles repeat, your child starts learning self-discipline and time management, core skills invaluable for ADHD children (Josel, 2022). Set a timer for 25 minutes; during this time, it's all systems go on studying. This short burst creates a sense of urgency, but it's not so long that your child feels discouraged. It's imperative that after the buzzer, they take a full 5-minute break—no cheating! This downtime is a blessing, giving their brain a chance to reset and digest the information.

Mind Mapping

Mind maps are perfect for turning monotonous note-taking into something creative and engaging. Encourage them to draw their notes in colorful diagrams that branch out from a central idea. This method plays to the strengths of the ADHD brain, which often processes information visually and non-linearly. By connecting concepts with images and pathways, mind maps facilitate better memory retention and understanding (*Mind Mapping*, 2023). They make abstract or complex information tangible and can be especially powerful for subjects that involve relationships between topics. By creating and reviewing their mind maps, your child is actively engaging with the material, making it more memorable and easier to recall during tests or class discussions.

Flashcards

Flashcards harness the power of active recall, a process where the brain retrieves information from memory rather than passively reviewing it (Holmes, 2023). This technique strengthens memory retention and makes studying more interactive. Guide your child to create flashcards with a question on one side and the answer on the other. When they flip the card to check if they got it right, it reinforces learning through self-assessment. Flashcards are incredibly versatile; they can be used for vocabulary, historical dates, math formulas, and more. Even creating the cards is a learning process itself, as it involves summarizing and condensing information into bite-sized pieces. Plus, the cards are portable, so kids can squeeze in quick review sessions anywhere, which is perfect for an ADHD mind that might struggle with long study periods.

Mnemonics

Mnemonic devices are clever tricks for remembering by linking complex information to simple words, phrases, or visual cues (Heerema, 2022). Sit down together and create mnemonics for tricky concepts or processes. For example, remember the order of operations in math with the phrase "Please Excuse My Dear Aunt Sally," representing Parentheses, Exponents, Multiplication, Division, Addition, and Subtraction. You don't have to use this exact example, but it's shortcuts like these that'll give your child's brain a hook to grab onto, something that transforms abstract information into tangible and memorable cues. Plus, mnemonics work particularly well for ADHD children as they often have creative and visual minds that can latch onto these imaginative cues more easily than memorizing by heart. (Lastiri, 2023).

Color Coding

Color-coding leverages the ADHD tendency toward visual learning to categorize and prioritize information. Get them to use different colored pens, highlighters, or sticky notes to organize their notes and materials. For example, use blue for vocabulary words, green for formulas, and yellow for key dates. Besides making their notes more visually appealing, it also helps them separate and recall information more easily (Diachenko et al., 2022).

Practice Tests

For a realistic simulation of test conditions, use practice tests to help them get accustomed to the format and timing of exams. As an active learning tool, practice tests force your child to recall information from memory, apply concepts, and think critically about approaching questions (TestPrepTraining, 2019). For ADHD children who have issues with focus, practice tests are a clear and defined challenge to tackle; in this way, their study time is goal-oriented and efficient.

Study techniques for ADHD kids revolve around making learning stick, but without regular breaks, that new knowledge might just bounce off. Think of breaks as the glue between study sessions; they help these strategies set and hold so their focus is fresh and their mind ready for more.

Taking Regular Breaks

Imagine trying to run a marathon without any rest stops; you'd burn out fast, right? ADHD brains are like high-powered engines that overheat without a cool-down. Regular breaks let them recharge and come back to their work with fresh eyes and renewed focus.

Taking breaks isn't wasted time; they're essential for maintaining stamina and productivity (Dolin, 2023). During study sessions, a break can be the difference between information sticking and slipping through the cracks. By doing so, the brain can process and store the learned information. For ADHD children, who may find sustained attention challenging, these breaks are even more critical. They give a necessary release for energy and restlessness, which reduces frustration and increases the likelihood of a productive study session (Kneisler, 2023). So, when you encourage your child to take regular breaks, you're not just helping them study better; you're helping them learn how to manage their attention and energy levels!

COMING UP

As you build on getting those study techniques up and running while giving your child those much-needed breaks to cement their learning, success isn't just about acing tests; it's also about feeling good and connecting with others. Social skills and self-esteem are huge; they let your kid shine not just in the classroom but out on the playground, too. Up next, we're getting into the nitty-gritty of how you can help your ADHD superstar build friendships and confidence. Let's get those social skills and self-esteem soaring!

7

ENHANCING SOCIAL SKILLS AND BUILDING SELF-ESTEEM

A recent study from 2018 suggests that kids with ADHD have higher rates of peer rejection, make fewer friends, and are less socially active compared to children without the diagnosis (Aduen et al., 2018).

They might say or do things without thinking, leading to misunderstandings or conflicts with their peers. It's tough when you feel like you don't fit in or are constantly left out. The lack of social connections can further exacerbate the issue. With fewer friends, they may miss out on important social experiences and opportunities for growth, and if they feel isolated or lonely, it can take a toll on their self-esteem (Mandriota, 2022). They might start doubting their worth and abilities, thinking that something is wrong with them. A limited range of social activities can also get in the way of their ability to develop a diverse set of social skills. Socializing with different people and doing different things teaches them how to handle different social situations. Without these opportunities, it becomes harder for them to interact meaningfully with others.

STRATEGY 13: NURTURING SOCIAL INTERACTION SKILLS

A social life like this sounds scary, but don't lose hope just yet; together, we can create a nurturing environment where your child can flourish socially and emotionally. Keep believing in them, and with some strategies to enhance social skills and self-esteem under your belt, you can help them find their place in the world. The first thing to look at is the different ways in which ADHD affects children socially:

- Imagine a kid's birthday party, and while others are connecting over games, an ADHD child impulsively interrupts or can't wait their turn. It's not that they don't get the rules; it's that their brain's impulse control is a bit hit-and-miss. It's frustrating, sure, but it's ADHD in action, not a defiant personality.
- Then, there's the group project scene in science class. An ADHD child's ideas are popping like fireworks, but they blurt them out and dominate the discussion, not picking up on the eye rolls from classmates. They're not trying to be

overbearing; their ADHD brain is just set to broadcast mode without the listen function fully tuned in.

- Let's not forget texting. While other teens decode social cues and emojis with ease, an ADHD teen might misread the tone, reply in a rush, and send messages that miss the mark. It's not insensitivity; it's their brain's social radar that needs a bit of fine-tuning.

These are glimpses of how ADHD can play out in social settings, but they're not insurmountable. Knowing what ADHD traits to target with your strategies will go a long way in helping your child improve socially. Why? For these kids, every friendship made, every game played together, it's more than just fun; it's key to their growth. From making friends to working in teams, these are the skills we need to connect with others, express ourselves, and deal with social situations (Cooks-Campbell, 2022). Think beyond today, too. These skills are their armor for the social battlefield of teenage years and adulthood. Being able to connect with others affects everything: school projects, job interviews, and relationships.

The Impact of Social Skills on Self-Esteem

Think of a child sharing laughs, joining games, and making friends; that's social skills in action. Now, see that grin on their face? That's self-esteem blooming. Every "you're so funny," every invite to hang out, it's like a vote of confidence. They start thinking, "Hey, I'm pretty awesome," and believe it, too. On the other hand, imagine a child struggling to jump into a conversation or can't quite catch the rhythm of a group chat; it stings. They might start to feel invisible, or worse, like there's something wrong with them. That's where self-esteem can take a hit. It's tough watching other kids sail smoothly in social situations while feeling like they're barely getting by.

But when kids get the hang of social skills, it's transformative. They're like social experts, reading cues and knowing when to speak up or listen. Every successful interaction is like a mini-win, and those wins stack up. Self-esteem soars because they're part of the tribe; they're in on the joke, and they're doing well socially (Araujo, 2023).

TECHNIQUES FOR TEACHING AND REINFORCING POSITIVE SOCIAL INTERACTIONS

It's a simple equation: good social skills equal positive interactions, and positive interactions pump up self-esteem. A sense of belonging comes from feeling valued, capable, and connected, and this is the kind of math we want our kids to ace. Here's how you can help:

Role Playing

Role-playing is like a social skills lab right in your living room. You create scenarios that mimic real-life situations where they need to handle conversations, share, wait their turn, and deal with conflicts. It's hands-on learning, and hands-on is key for kids with ADHD.

Telling a child what to do is one thing, but letting them practice it? That's when it sticks. Role-playing gives them a safe space to mess up, learn, and try again without real-world pressure. Plus, it's interactive and fun, which keeps their attention (we know that's half the battle). And the best part is you're right there to guide them. If they slip up, you're showing them how to fix it, not just what went wrong. It's real-time feedback, and for an ADHD brain, that's ideal; they learn the cause and effect of social interactions on the spot.

Tips for Setting up Role-Playing Scenarios:

- Keep it simple and start with everyday situations like sharing toys or choosing a TV show. This makes it relatable and easier for your child to grasp.
- Throw in some props, like a stuffed animal for a pretend tea party or a board game for turn-taking practice. Props are great for making the scenario feel real while keeping it low-stakes.
- Keep your scenarios short and sweet; ADHD kids can find it demanding to focus for long periods, so a quick five-minute play session can do wonders without losing their attention.
- Take turns playing different roles to help them see things from different perspectives; make it so one minute you're the shopkeeper, the next you're the customer, and vice versa.
- Use real-life consequences to explain if they snatch a toy, pause, and discuss how that might make their friend feel and what a better approach could be.
- If they make a social blunder, keep it light and use it as a teachable moment. Guide them through what could be done differently next time.

Scenario 1: Sharing and Taking Turns

Play a game that your child enjoys but struggles to play without interrupting; this works best with a board game, card game, or anything else that involves waiting and taking turns. Before starting, discuss the rules of turn-taking and how important it is to let others have theirs. Role-play a few rounds, where you deliberately take extra time on your turn. Encourage your child to practice patience by counting to 10 or giving a compliment while they wait.

Example:

- You: "It's my turn now. I'm going to roll the dice and move my piece. Hmm, let me think about this move carefully."
- Your child: (Waits, counting to 10)
- After the role-play, discuss how it felt to wait and remind them that it wasn't worth getting upset over.

Scenario 2: Expressing Feelings

Role-play a situation where your child needs to express how they feel about something without raising their voice or getting upset. Practice using "I feel" statements and finding solutions together.

Example:

- You: "When you took my toy without asking, I felt sad."
- Your child: "I feel sorry for taking it. Next time, I'll ask first. Can we play together now?"

Scenario 3: Dealing With Conflict

Prepare a setup where a common conflict arises, like a disagreement over which TV show to watch. Guide your child through the steps of addressing the conflict, using calm words, and finding a compromise.

Example:

- You: "I see we both want to watch something different on TV. I want to watch a documentary, and you want to watch a cartoon."
- Your child: "Yeah, I really want to watch my cartoon."
- You: "Let's find a way to make it fair. How about we watch one episode of your cartoon, then one episode of my cooking show?"

Scenario 4: Managing Interruptions

During a family conversation, practice a signal that means "wait for your turn to talk." When they want to say something, they use the signal, and you acknowledge them but remind them to wait until whoever's speaking is finished.

Example:

- Sibling: "Today at school, we had a science fair and..."
- Your child raises their hand or uses another agreed-upon signal.
- You: "I see you have something to add, but let your brother finish his story first, and then it's your turn."

Scenario 5: Active Listening

Play a storytelling game where your child needs to listen carefully and then repeat the main points of the story.

Example:

- You: "Once upon a time, there was a rabbit who loved to race. He challenged a turtle to a race, thinking he would win easily."
- After the story, your child: "The rabbit raced the turtle because he thought he'd win, but the turtle had a trick up his sleeve!"

Throughout these exercises, give immediate and specific feedback to keep them motivated and engaged. Say things like, "I liked how you asked for a turn," or "You did a great job listening."

Social Stories

With social stories, you're crafting short, personalized stories that give your child a heads-up on what to expect in certain situations and how to handle them. You're breaking down complex social cues into easy-to-digest, step-by-step narratives.

- You start by pinpointing a scenario your child struggles with. Say, playing fair.
- You then create a story with a character they can relate to, facing the same issue.
- The story walks through the emotions engaged, the expected behaviors, and the positive outcomes of playing fair.

Social stories can tackle anything from making friends to apologizing. It all comes down to tailoring the story to the social complications your child has. The more you use them, the more they'll get the hang of reading social signals and responding appropriately. The great thing here is it's not just telling them what to do; it's showing them the why behind it. It gives them a chance to mentally rehearse social situations in a no-pressure environment.

By the time they're in the thick of it, they've got a game plan, and that's a confidence booster.

Tips for Creating Social Stories:

- Start with a clear goal by identifying what social skill or situation you want to address. Is it keeping frustrations under wraps, taking turns, or saying "please" and "thank you"? Keep it focused to avoid overwhelming your child.
- Write it from their perspective using simple language and a first-person point of view. "I wait for my turn to play the video game" is direct and easy for them to relate to.
- Illustrate your story with pictures or drawings to show the emotions and actions involved; if you're talking about waiting patiently, show a calm face and a relaxed body posture.
- Include the why and explain the reasons behind certain social rules, say, "When I wait for my turn, everyone has fun," to help them recognize the benefit of their actions.
- Role-play the story after reading it so they can practice the behavior in a safe setting before trying it out in the real world.
- Read the social story regularly, especially before events where the skill will be needed; repetition reinforces learning (CPD, 2022).

- Update the stories as your child grows and their social understanding evolves because what works for a seven-year-old might not cut it for a teenager.
- Wrap up each session with encouragement, no matter how small, to motivate them to keep working on their social skills.

Storytime:

Write a story with your child as the main character, who gets over-excited and interrupts during class. Describe how the character feels when they have a cool idea, the buzz of wanting to share it, but also the frowns when they jump in. The story goes on to show the main character learning to raise their hand and wait; they feel proud when they do it right, and their classmates smile, giving them a thumbs up. For a real-world spin, next time you're in a conversation and they butt in, gently remind them, "Remember what our main character learned?" It's like a code between you two, nudging them to practice patience without the embarrassment.

This isn't a one-and-done deal; keep at it, regularly updating the stories to match new stories to things they struggle with:

- Craft a short story where the character faces a decision to share or not. Show both outcomes; sharing leads to a fun game with friends, not sharing results in playing alone. This way, your child sees the pros of positive behavior.

- Next, deal with meltdowns or social mishaps they struggle with. Create a tale about a kid feeling overwhelmed in class. Walk through the polite way to wait for the right moment, ask the teacher for a time out, and then highlight what happens when they have an outburst in front of their peers.

To get the most out of these stories, review them before an actual event. If you're heading to a group setting, read a story about manners to set up expectations, like a game plan before the big match. Then, after the event, have a debrief. Did they remember what happened in the story and try to model the character in real life? Praise the good stuff, talk about hiccups, and keep it positive.

Making and Keeping Friends

ADHD kids, just like others, thrive on friendships that make them feel good and like they belong. When they connect with peers, the connection sharpens their social skills through real-time practice, which is essential for emotional and psychological growth. You'll see them interpret social cues and learn to manage their impulses better in a social context. Additionally, friends are like a support system, giving your child a safe place to express themselves and feel understood. This companionship can also reduce feelings of isolation or difference they might feel because of their ADHD. Here's how you can help them make and keep friends:

- Encourage them to join clubs or activities they're passionate about. Being in a group with similar interests can make initiating conversations and forming connections easier for them.
- Practice common social scenarios at home, like the role-playing and social story exercises above.
- Notice and praise their social successes, no matter how trivial they seem. This boosts their confidence and reinforces good behavior.
- Encourage playdates, but keep them small. One-on-one is less overwhelming than a crowd, and it's easier to keep track of how things are going.
- Make sure your child knows the importance of listening to others. Remind them that friendships are a two-way street and understanding friends' feelings is key.
- Discuss feelings and empathy using books or shows to point out characters' emotions and ask how they'll feel in those situations.
- Kids learn by example, so show them how to keep eye contact, use polite language, and be attentive.
- Remind them that building friendships takes time; they don't need to rush things or feel discouraged if it doesn't happen immediately.

- Teach them to recognize and respond to bullying. Make sure they know if it happens to them, that it's not their fault, and they should always talk to you or another adult they trust.

STRATEGY 14: ACTIVITIES TO BOOST CONFIDENCE AND SELF-WORTH

ADHD often makes kids feel frustrated, overwhelmed, and inadequate, so finding activities where they can feel successful and recognize their own abilities can make all the difference. When they accomplish something they thought was impossible, whether it's scoring a goal, acing a spelling bee, or excelling in a hobby, it's a job well done moment, a true source of confidence (Williamson, 2021).

It's not just about the win; it's the journey toward the win that's loaded with value. When kids take part in activities they succeed in, it does wonders for how they see themselves because it gives them tangible proof of their abilities. It shifts their perspective from focusing on their challenges to acknowledging their strengths. Every time they achieve something, it's like a little mental note that says, *Hey, I can do this*. It's building blocks for confidence because they start to string together these achievements, and, hey presto, you've got a self-assured youngster who's ready to take on the world. But let's not forget about the sense of self-worth. When kids realize they're capable and competent, they learn their actions have more weight than praise (Greene, 2023). Better still, these activities encourage a positive mindset, teaching them the value of perseverance and hard work. When they see the direct correlation between effort and success, they learn they have control over how things turn out. This empowers them to take on challenges with a can-do attitude, knowing they can overcome obstacles. On the other side of this, there is no sense of achievement. That's when doubts creep in, *Am I good enough? Do I matter?* Those are heavy questions for tiny shoulders and why achievement-oriented activities are non-negotiable, the antidote to doubt.

Dive into this collection of creative and physical activities perfect for discovering what makes your little one tick. From painting masterpieces to climbing jungle gyms, there's a world of possibilities where kids can explore, experiment, and find their spark.

For the Creatives:

- **Goal journaling:** Grab a notebook and have them jot down goals, big or small, even a simple to-do list for the day. Each achieved goal gets a proud tick to hammer home the "I can do it" attitude.
- **Music lessons:** Whether it's banging on drums or strumming a guitar, music sharpens the brain, builds discipline, boosts self-esteem, and could even unveil a hidden Mozart.

- **Packing:** Let them pack their own bag for a day trip or school. They call the shots on what's essential, giving them a sense of control and responsibility. It's a simple task, but it tells them, "You've got this," reinforcing their decision-making skills and independence.
- **Photography:** Giving them a camera lets them capture the world through their lens, focusing attention and seeing beauty in the details.
- **Gardening:** Planting seeds and watching them grow teaches responsibility and the cycle of life.
- **Writing stories or poems:** It encourages language skills and can be a powerful outlet for emotions.
- **Volunteering:** Find age-appropriate community service that resonates with their interests; it's emotionally and mentally rewarding and socially enriching.

For the Adventurous:

- **Dance classes:** Whether ballet, hip-hop, or folk dance, it's a fun way to express creativity and build physical coordination.
- **Swimming:** It's a whole-body workout to build strength and endurance, as well as social skills.
- **Gymnastics:** Develops flexibility, balance, and incredible body strength.
- **Rock climbing:** Indoor or outdoor; it challenges problem-solving skills and builds confidence.

- **Cycling:** Offers a sense of freedom and adventure while improving stamina and cognitive function.
- **Horseback riding**: Teaches responsibility and builds a bond with animals.
- **Track and field:** Encourages personal goal setting and resilience.

As you can see, there are a lot of activities you can get your child involved in to develop their confidence and self-worth while also setting them up for some seriously productive life skills. Each activity can uncover a passion or talent, and along the way, they'll learn about teamwork, persistence, and the joy of success. Encourage them to try different things and see what sticks; the goal is to enjoy the process and celebrate any success.

Celebrating Small Successes to Build Confidence

These small successes might seem ordinary, but for your child, they are milestones; each one is a building block toward confidence (Slade, 2023). By celebrating these moments, you're cheering on good behavior; yes, but you're also reinforcing their competence and boosting their self-esteem. You don't need to show grand gestures; a simple "I'm proud of you" does wonders. Whether they get involved with a new activity, socialize in a group sport, or sit down and plow through their homework without a reminder, these are the times to celebrate! And don't forget those moments when they remember their chores without a nudge from you. Praise their memory skills and responsibility; this is them showing independence and growth, attributes that are clear as day and signal self-worth. Here's how to get things going:

- **Set clear goals:** Start with small, achievable goals they can reach easily, like reading a short book or a ten-minute focus session. This gives them frequent opportunities to succeed and feel proud.
- **Routine rewards:** Establish a routine where you recognize achievements regularly, whether it's with verbal praise or a reward system.
- **Focus on strengths:** ADHD kids often hear about their struggles, so emphasize and praise what they're good at, whether it's creativity, energy, or being a good friend.
- **Active listening:** A great way to validate their self-worth is to show them you care about their feelings and thoughts by giving them your full attention when they speak.
- **Encourage physical activity:** Sports or dance improves focus, provides structure, and enhances self-esteem.
- **Offer choices:** Let them make decisions within a set range of options to encourage independence and confidence in their decision-making.
- **Teach problem-solving:** Instead of swooping in to fix every issue, guide them through solving problems to build resilience and self-reliance.

- **Create a success portfolio:** Keep a folder of their achievements, big and small, to remind them of their progress.
- **Model positive self-talk:** Be mindful of how you talk about yourself and any issues you're going through as an adult; kids learn by example.

Every one of these tips is a step toward building a confident child. Remember, your belief in them powers their belief in themselves. So, keep the focus on progress, not perfection, and celebrate all victories as they come. As you do this, it's like a confidence domino effect; they're now primed to jump into group activities and hobbies with gusto. This leap from individual accomplishments to thriving in a team setting is great for weaving their newfound self-worth into the rich tapestry of social skills and shared experiences.

STRATEGY 15: ENCOURAGING INVOLVEMENT IN GROUP ACTIVITIES AND HOBBIES

Jumping into group activities and hobbies, your child taps into a vibrant strategy where teamwork and social skills blossom naturally. Picture this: they're on a soccer team, and every pass of the ball teaches them about collaboration and anticipating others' needs. Or they're in a drama club, where each rehearsal is a lesson in empathy as they step into different characters' shoes. In a robotics team, they learn to communicate ideas clearly and listen, key social skills for all children. And think about a cooking class, where timing and coordination are the secret ingredients to a successful dish, subtly schooling them in the art of working in harmony. These aren't just hobbies; they're life lessons where ADHD kids learn to read social cues, wait their turn, and value others' contributions, all while the fun keeps them hooked and the shared goals bond them with peers. It's in these groups they find their tribe, practice patience, and discover that wins are sweeter when celebrated together.

So, encourage your child to get involved in activities with their peers because they're not just playing; they're growing:

- **Board game nights:** Grab some classic board games or the latest strategy games and invite your child and their friends over. Playing games teaches kids to be strategic thinkers and gracious winners or losers, all in a fun setting.
- **Building block clubs:** Great for younger kids, either in a club setting or at home, this activity involves setting up challenges where they construct specific structures within a time limit. It's a hands-on activity that enhances environmental orientation, creativity, and problem-solving.
- **Agricultural clubs:** With a local 4-H club or a school gardening project, they'll learn about

cultivating plants, caring for animals, and appreciating nature. These activities encourage responsibility and patience, boosting self-esteem as they witness the growth and results of their dedication.

- **Scouting groups:** Scouting activities promote teamwork, leadership, and problem-solving. Your child can earn badges and take on new challenges while building a sense of achievement and self-reliance. Plus, outdoor adventures can instill a lifelong appreciation for nature and personal growth.
- **Academic clubs:** Sign your child up for a debate team, math league, or science club. These groups challenge kids intellectually, give them a sense of achievement, and enhance public speaking skills.
- **Coding clubs:** Coding is the future, with jobs expected to grow 21% by 2028, a rate much higher than other careers (Massimine, 2023). They'll learn to build and troubleshoot their own programs, a skill that not only taps into problem-solving but also gives a sense of accomplishment as they see their code come to life.
- **Robotics clubs:** Hands-on building and programming robots tackle complex tasks and work in teams. When they successfully complete challenges with their robot, they'll learn teamwork and technical skills, as well as resilience

when debugging, which strengthens their self-esteem.

Now, how can you get your child involved in these activities and find the ones that resonate with their interests and strengths?

- Notice what makes your child's eyes light up. Is it when they're drawing, having fun in a team, or retelling stories? Use these cues to guide hobby choices. Say they sketch all day; art classes could be a hit. They'll learn techniques and the value of feedback, increasing their skills and self-confidence.
- Start small and encourage them to try different activities on a trial basis before committing to anything long-term. This will give them the chance to explore their options without feeling overwhelmed.
- Make hobbies accessible by keeping art supplies within easy reach or a skateboard near the door. The goal is to remove barriers to their interests because accessibility encourages spontaneous engagement. For example, a telescope in their room can spur nightly stargazing if they're into astronomy.
- Fit the hobby to their energy levels; some ADHD kids have an abundance of energy, so something that involves physical exertion could be ideal.

- Find groups or clubs with a supportive and inclusive environment for children with ADHD. Being part of a community with shared interests will make them comfortable enough to socialize and get involved more.

COMING UP

So, as we wrap this up, remember that boosting social skills and self-esteem in kids with ADHD goes beyond structured activities. Yes, finding activities they enjoy is great for making friends and feeling good about themselves, but your approach should extend to everything they do. From the classroom to the playground and home, a holistic approach to these strategies and the others we've covered weave together to build a comprehensive support system, each thread strengthening the others. Let's now turn to creating a comprehensive support system aimed at helping them grow while making sure they have all the tools they need to shine in every aspect of their lives.

8

INTEGRATING STRATEGIES FOR HOLISTIC APPROACH

No one can whistle a symphony. It takes a whole orchestra to play it.

— H.E. LUCCOCK

RECAP OF KEY STRATEGIES

This quote nails the power of teamwork. Just like an orchestra's blend of instruments creates a symphony, nurturing an ADHD child's growth is a coordinated effort. You're trying different coping strategies, seeing what works and what doesn't, while syncing with teachers, therapists, and family to hit the right notes in social skills and self-esteem.

So, if you're the conductor, orchestrating this symphony of strategies to support your ADHD child, let's recap the key techniques that'll help you tune in to what works best for them.

- **Strategy 1: Recognizing ADHD Symptoms and Behaviors:** Stepping into your child's world, you understand the why behind actions that might seem puzzling. This means seeing the world through their unique lens, not conforming to labeling like "difficult" or "distracted."
- **Strategy 2: Exploring the Neurological Underpinnings of ADHD:** By exploring the neurological underpinnings of ADHD, you discover the science behind the condition, not just how to manage it. This knowledge empowers you to tailor your approach, aligning with how your child's brain operates and responds to the environment.
- **Strategy 3: Active Listening Techniques:** Active listening goes beyond just listening; with this, you're fully engaging with their thoughts and feelings. It's a powerful tool for building trust and creating a strong bond by showing them that you care about what they think and feel.
- **Strategy 4: Understanding Nonverbal Cues and Communication Strategies:** Children with ADHD often communicate more through actions than words, and understanding nonverbal cues takes you beyond words; by tuning into these

signals, you're connecting on a deeper level, bridging gaps where words fall short.

- **Strategy 5: Positive Reinforcement and Encouragement:** More than a mere present, positive reinforcement and encouragement are a consistent boost to your child's self-esteem. When you focus on what they do right, you're lighting up pathways to confidence and motivation, key ingredients for handling ADHD challenges.

- **Strategy 6: Establishing Clear Boundaries and Consistent Rules:** With clear boundaries and consistent rules, you're creating a predictable structure to help them understand expectations. Within defined limits, this clarity reduces confusion and encourages growth.

- **Strategy 7: Establishing an ADHD-Friendly Home Environment:** An ADHD-friendly home environment focuses on minimizing distractions and creating a focus-enhancing environment. You're designing a living space to support rather than hinder their unique demands.

- **Strategy 8: Family Nutrition and Self-Care:** Family nutrition and self-care aren't just health lingo; they're foundational for managing ADHD. Balanced diets and regular exercise enhance energy and focus, while self-care routines mean they're feeling good and you're at your best when supporting them.

- **Strategy 9: Teaching Self-Regulation Techniques:** Teaching self-regulation techniques will help your child better manage their emotions and impulses. You're empowering them to take control, which is incredibly affirming and builds resilience.

- **Strategy 10: Techniques for Calming and De-escalation:** Critical during heightened moments, with calming and de-escalation techniques, you're able to gently guide them back into calm, reducing stress and learning to manage intense emotions.

- **Strategy 11: Collaborating With Educators for Accommodations:** Collaborating with educators gets you and the school on the same page. You're the integral link to harmonizing home and school strategies to ensure your child gets the necessary accommodations to succeed academically.

- **Strategy 12: Establishing Effective Study Habits:** Developing study habits that stick helps your child handle assignments with focus and less frustration. Making study time productive and less stressful is about smart strategies for learning, not spending more time at the desk.

- **Strategy 13: Nurturing Social Interaction Skills:** Developing social skills prepares your child for friendships and group settings. You're guiding them to understand social cues and respond appropriately, which is essential for building relationships.

- **Strategy 14: Activities to Boost Confidence and Self-Worth:** Show your child they're more than their ADHD by involving them in activities that boost confidence and self-worth. You're helping them discover their strengths and acknowledge their successes to develop a strong sense of self.
- **Strategy 15: Encouraging Involvement in Group Activities and Hobbies:** Getting kids involved in group activities and hobbies will give them a sense of belonging and encourage them to work together. Here, you're channeling their energy into positive experiences where they can shine and connect with others who share their interests.

CREATING A COHESIVE PLAN

Mastering these strategies is just the start; the real secret to success is integrating them seamlessly into your everyday hustle. When you start syncing these tactics with daily routines, you create a rhythm that makes consistency less of a battle and more of a natural part of life.

- You kick off the morning with a healthy, balanced breakfast; think brain food from strategy 8, balancing proteins and carbs to begin the day on the right foot.
- Start with a morning reminder from strategy 6: clear boundaries. Over breakfast, you remind

them of what's expected: simple, concrete rules like "We brush our teeth after eating."

- As they gear up for school, strategy 11 comes into play. You've chatted with their teacher about accommodations—maybe a quieter desk spot or extra time with the teacher for longer assignments —and you remind them these are in place to help them succeed.
- After school, it's homework time. Strategy 12 comes in here. You've created a focus area and a simple task list so they know exactly what to study and when.
- Then, you transition to strategy 13: nurturing social skills. Maybe you role-play a conversation or encourage them to call a friend, reinforcing those essential interaction skills.
- For a breather, strategy 7 takes the stage. Your home is their haven, organized, quiet corners for chill time, and everything's labeled to help them find stuff easily.
- Dinnertime is ideal for strategy 8 again, where you talk about the day's wins while munching on brain-friendly foods, think omega-3s and whole grains.
- As the day winds down, you slip into strategies 9 and 10, teaching self-regulation and calming techniques. Maybe it's a few yoga poses or deep-breathing exercises before bedtime.

- Don't forget strategies 14 and 15 throughout the day. Focus on their strengths with activities they excel at, boosting confidence, and plug them into group hobbies where they shine and learn teamwork, like a solo hobby or soccer practice.

There you have it, a day packed with targeted strategies all geared toward healthy behavior as well as academic and social success.

But let's not forget that not every strategy sticks the same for every child; you have to play to the rhythm of your family. Let's look at how you can cherry-pick and rank these strategies to hit the sweet spot for your child's one-of-a-kind needs.

- If your child is the type to be dynamic in the morning but fizzle out by noon, you could prioritize strategy 12, establishing effective study habits during their peak hours. Have them work on the toughest homework when they're most alert, and save lighter tasks for the slump time.
- For social butterflies, strategy 13 works to enhance social interaction skills. Playdates become prime time to coach them on sharing and taking turns.
- If they're getting the hang of it, switch gears to strategy 14, setting up confidence-boosting activities. Perhaps they've really got into

journaling; set up an art station with coloring pens, stickers, and other scrapbook supplies where they can create and display their work.

- If their nonverbal communication is unclear, give strategy 4 some attention. Spend time observing their gestures or facial expressions and gently guide them on how to read others.
- When things get heated, strategy 10 for calming and de-escalation is your go-to. Have a toolkit of chill-out tricks ready; maybe playing with a fidget tool, deep breathing, or snuggling into a quiet corner with a good book.
- Strategy 6—setting clear boundaries and rules—is your backbone. It's about daily reinforcement and giving them stability so they know what to expect.
- Collaborating with educators for accommodations, from strategy 6, is ongoing. Stay in sync with teachers to tweak learning plans as your child's abilities change.

Mix and match these strategies like you're crafting a custom recipe to help your child succeed because the approach that works today might need tweaking tomorrow, and that's okay. You're tuning into their needs, keeping the best rhythm for them.

As you fine-tune the strategies you use every day, always remember you're not alone. Having a support network of teachers, therapists, and fellow parents will be invaluable in helping you and your child.

BUILDING A SUPPORT NETWORK

You know that raising a kid with ADHD isn't easy; it's complex and ever-changing. That's where a support network comes in. This is your tribe, the folks who get the highs and lows because they're right there with you.

Think about it; when you're stumped on homework strategies, an educator in your corner can offer tailored techniques. Or when you're frazzled by a meltdown, a therapist can provide de-escalation tactics that work. And let's be real; sometimes, you just need to vent. Family and friends who get it and are the ones you lean on when you need a break or just a listening ear. They can step in to babysit or help with homework, giving you that much-needed breather. They're your cheerleaders, encouraging you and helping dust you off when there's a stumble. Then, there's the power of shared experiences. Online groups and forums are a 24/7 resource where you can swap stories, ask for advice, or vent at 2 a.m. to someone across the globe who's also up with a restless kid. They're a goldmine of advice, and sometimes, the best life hacks come from someone five time zones away.

No matter who you've got in your corner, building a support network is more than getting help; you're building a community that understands the rollercoaster you're on. They can offer practical tips, sure, but they also get the emotional side of things, too. They can be there as your sounding board, your advisors, and your cheerleaders, the ones who remind you that you're not alone. So, reach out, connect, and build that safety net; it's one of the smartest moves you'll make.

Once you've got your crew assembled, you'll also need to constantly monitor and adapt your strategies to keep them as dynamic as your child's needs. Here, you're pinpointing what's clicking and what needs a nudge so your approach stays sharp and effective.

MONITORING AND ADAPTING

Keeping a calendar or writing down things helps you see patterns. Maybe your child is super focused right after a run outside, or maybe homework before dinner is a no-go. This information helps build a routine around their peak focus times. And when you spot areas for improvement, you're not guessing; you have data guiding you to the right strategies, like adding more breaks or trying out a new organizational tool.

When you monitor and adapt, you're tracking progress; you want to know how far you've come, what works, and what doesn't. Luckily, this doesn't mean nitpicking every little thing you do; think of it as gathering intel to help you make better decisions:

- Log daily behaviors, achievements, and challenges to highlight patterns. Say they're nailing emotional regulation skills on Tuesdays; with your journal, you spot the trend: It's the day after your chill-out Mondays. Bingo, you've got a connection.
- Keep their report cards and teacher's notes handy. These are like snapshots of your child's academic journey. When you see a dip or a spike, you get clues on where to focus.
- Don't forget any parent-teacher meetings. Teachers see your child in a different light, so they can flag up stuff you might not see at home.
- Regular check-ins with healthcare professionals can measure growth against milestones and help tweak your methods or therapies as needed.

However, you track their progress and identify areas for improvement; don't think of it as a test. Think of it as a tool for customizing your ADHD strategy and fitting it around how your child behaves and what they need to do better. Because as they grow, so too does the landscape of their needs. Like walking through a city where the streets are always changing, what worked at one intersection may not apply at the next.

Be Flexible and Adaptable

In the early years, you might have strategies revolving around simple routines and clear, immediate rewards. But as they hit new developmental milestones, those tactics may lose their shine. The preteen years come with all kinds of social dynamics and a growing sense of independence. Here, your approach must evolve to include conversations about self-awareness and self-regulation. Adolescence throws in another twist with a quest for identity and autonomy. Now, success strategies hinge on collaboration rather than direction. You're no longer just the rule-setter; you're a guide on the side, helping them find their own path. Flexibility means recalibrating your expectations and adapting the support you offer to align with your evolving sense of self.

ADHD is not a static condition; it's a nuanced and multi-layered part of your child that'll change as they grow older. Being flexible to this and adapting as they grow is the key to unlocking their potential at every stage of life.

LONG-TERM GOALS AND EXPECTATIONS

As you tweak your strategies in real-time, you're also setting the stage for the long haul, grounding your expectations in the reality of your child's life with ADHD. By doing so, you're not just tinkering with daily challenges;

you're carving out a path toward meaningful progress and long-term wins.

As a parent, you know by now that your child has to deal with some extra challenges not faced by their peers, so it's tempting to either set the bar sky-high or keep it too low out of fear of failure. But here's the deal: setting realistic expectations and long-term goals is a great strategy to assess their current status and plot a course for where they can realistically aspire to be. To do this, you must have realistic expectations guiding them through the rough terrain of daily tasks without setting them up for a fall. This means striking that sweet spot between challenging and achievable by taking incremental steps to build confidence and competence. You're essentially teaching them the art of progress, not perfection. Long-term goals, on the other hand, are the North Star of your child's future; they give direction and purpose. For a child with ADHD, these goals should be flexible, allowing for a scenic route rather than a straight path to success. These goals are less about the endpoint and more about developing resilience and adaptability, the courage to face life's challenges head-on, turning "I can't" into "I just haven't yet."

Be Patient and Persevere

As you guide them through their life like this, use patience as your steady pace and perseverance as your stride. You'll need to accept that progress for your ADHD child often looks like a series of small leaps rather than giant bounds. It's okay to embrace the subtle shifts, the tantrum that lasts a little less, the school bag packed without a reminder. These moments are priceless, the building blocks of a larger triumph. ADHD management is an intricate puzzle, and each little piece your child places is a victory. You're in this together, every step of the way, and when you hit a plateau or face a setback, remember it's just another stretch of road on this journey. Patience whispers, "This is tough, but we're tougher," perseverance responds, "We've got this, one step at a time." Progress is there in the patience it takes to work through a difficult problem and the perseverance to try again after a misstep. It's woven into the fabric of daily life, routines that eventually become second nature, and the coping strategies that turn into habits. Keep celebrating the minor changes because they add up to significant gains, including building the foundation for lifelong skills and resilience. Not only are you managing behaviors, you're nurturing growth, step by incremental step. Your patience and perseverance send a powerful message to your child: they are capable, they can manage their ADHD, and they can achieve great things, one small victory at a time.

This steady encouragement is the bedrock for teaching them to take the reins and recognize their strengths and how to use them. The key is to transition from your supportive role to them being their own advocate, confidently navigating the world with ADHD as their sidekick, not their kryptonite.

EMPOWERING YOUR CHILD

What happens when we encourage independence in our children? They become self-reliant and confident decision-makers. They learn to trust their judgment, take initiative, and handle the consequences of their actions (Gallo, 2023). Even for ADHD children, these are essential life skills needed to cope with the complexities of life. You, too, can instill this assurance in your child by:

- When it comes to decision-making, give them choices.

  - Whether it's picking out their clothes or deciding on a snack, each choice made is a step towards independence. It teaches them to trust their judgment and to understand the consequences of their decisions.
  - Encourage them to set their own goals, too. Maybe it's finishing a book or building a model; whatever it is, let them lead. They learn to drive their own projects, see them through, and revel

in the accomplishment.

- For self-advocacy—the language and confidence to express their needs and thoughts—try setting up different scenarios where they need to ask for help or stand up for themselves.

  o A good example would be talking to a teacher about a misunderstood assignment or negotiating more playtime. The important thing is they're doing the talking, not you.

- Encourage them to understand their ADHD, not as a flaw but as a unique aspect of themselves that they can explain to others.
- Teach them to articulate what they need to succeed.

  o Whether it's a time out when their head gets too loud or extra time to complete assignments.
  o Make sure they know they're nurturing a sense of self-respect by showing them that their voice matters and only they have the power to affect change in their world.

- Encourage a growth mindset to shift focus from a fixed "I can't" mentality to an "I can learn" approach. By encouraging a growth mindset, you teach them that their abilities aren't fixed. You're telling them that with effort and persistence, they can learn and improve, just like anyone else.

- ○ Tell them that every effort they make is a step towards mastering a skill, regardless of how many attempts it takes. This reassures them that it's okay to struggle and that perseverance is needed to overcome obstacles.

- So they'll see the value in what they're doing irrespective of the outcome, acknowledge and appreciate what they're doing, and emphasize the effectiveness of the strategies and the focus they apply to them, not just the end result.

Your guidance today is the foundation for their success tomorrow. Each struggle, each triumph, is a chance to instill a growth mindset. With every challenge you reframe as a chance to grow and every effort you praise, you're planting seeds for a resilient, adaptive, and confident mindset. You might be managing ADHD now, but ultimately, you're raising a future adult. An adult who knows how to organize their life, make decisions, and advocate for themselves: A truly empowered individual.

FINAL REFLECTIONS AND ENCOURAGEMENTS

The Effective ADHD Parenting Guide is a companion on your journey to becoming the effective, compassionate, and proactive parent your ADHD child needs. You are now armed with 15 powerhouse strategies to make this journey smoother. Some of the main points to remember are:

- Communication is a big deal here. You're learning to speak your child's language, and though it may feel like translating a secret language at times, every breakthrough is a triumph.
- When outbursts happen, and they will, you're prepared with the tools to handle them gracefully. This means you're not just reacting; you're responding with a strategic calm that promotes learning and growth for both of you.
- Reducing stress is not a luxury; it's a necessity, and your ability to stay composed is your superpower. It's okay to take a breather, step back, and care for yourself. Doing so isn't selfish; it's a necessity; a relaxed you is a more effective you.
- You're also encouraging resilience in your child, as well as in yourself. Each challenge is an opportunity to demonstrate that setbacks are not the end but a part of the learning curve. The goal

is to celebrate every milestone and recognize that each step forward is a collective success.

At the heart of it all, you're empowering your child. You're giving them the support to succeed in their unique way. Because guess what? You've got this parenting thing down. By embracing these practical, tried, and tested strategies, you will build a stress-free, harmonious relationship with your child. You're the confident, competent parent who gets it, who sees the world through your child's eyes and understands what they need to flourish.

You're finding that sweet spot, balancing pleasing your child and working in harmony with teachers and family members. Everyone's on the same team now and you're the anchor, promoting understanding and support beyond the home and into every aspect of your child's life. Always value structure and predictability, which brings comfort to the ADHD mind. This way, you build a solid routine, stand tall and impenetrable like a lighthouse against the storm, and guide your child toward self-regulation and emotional mastery.

This book isn't just a set of strategies; it's a source of hope, a reminder that ADHD doesn't define your child; it's just one part of their story. A page in which you're playing a huge role in raising them to be resilient, emotionally intelligent, and socially adept. The strategies within this book are your tools, and the results are clear: A family life where everyone feels confident, fulfilled, and connected.

Even if things don't go well, hold onto the courage to implement these strategies, have the resilience to keep going when it's tough, and the belief in your child's potential. You're not only managing ADHD; you're unlocking a world of possibilities for your child. So, keep pushing forward with love and determination, and know that you're not alone and you're more capable than you imagined.

As you're turning the pages of *The Effective ADHD Parenting Guide*, I'm curious about the chapters that are resonating with you. Those strategies for communication, are they working? And those tips for dealing with outbursts, finding them helpful? We need to support each other, and hearing how the book might be shaping your family's narrative could help other parents in similar situations. What's been your experience?

REFERENCES

Abdelnour, E., Jansen, M. O., & Gold, J. A. (2022). ADHD diagnostic trends: Increased recognition or overdiagnosis? *Missouri Medicine*, *119*(5), 467–473. https://www.ncbi.nlm.nih.gov/pmc/articles/PMC9616454/#:~

ADDRC. (2023, August 27). *Using visual cues to remember or retrieve information when You have ADHD – ADD Resource Center*. The A.D.D. Resource Center. https://www.addrc.org/using-visual-cues-to-remember-or-retrieve-information-when-you-have-adhd/#:~

Adejokun, M. (2020, November 11). *The importance of listening to children*. Childcare & Education Expo. https://childcareeducationexpo.co.uk/listening-to-children/

ADHD Group Approaches. (2023). *ADHD group approaches*. MentalHelp. https://www.mentalhelp.net/adhd/group-approaches/#:~:

Aduen, P. A., Day, T. N., Kofler, M. J., Harmon, S. L., Wells, E. L., & Sarver, D. E. (2018). Social problems in ADHD: Is it a skills acquisition or performance problem? *Journal of Psychopathology and Behavioral Assessment*, *40*(3), 440–451. https://doi.org/10.1007/s10862-018-9649-7

Alton, L. (2017, June 22). *Why clutter is killing your focus -- and how to fix it fast*. NBC News. https://www.nbcnews.com/better/health/why-clutter-killing-your-focus-how-fix-it-ncna775531

Araujo, G. (2023, September). *Your child's self-esteem (for parents)*. KidsHealth. https://kidshealth.org/en/parents/self-esteem.html#:~

Austin, D. (2023, July 4). *Houseplants for ADHD: How they help & how to keep them alive*. Getinflow. https://www.getinflow.io/post/houseplants-for-adhd-benefits-care-tips

Barkley, R. (2021, September 20). *DESR: Why deficient emotional self-regulation is central to ADHD (and largely overlooked)*. ADDitude. https://www.additudemag.com/desr-adhd-emotional-regulation/

Blackburn, S. (2021, October 13). *7 popular clubs and extracurricular activities for kids.* Verywell Family. https://www.verywellfamily. com/types-of-clubs-kids-and-youth-2087395

Borba, M. (2022, April 16). *A psychologist says these 7 skills separate successful kids from "the ones who struggle"—and how parents can teach them.* CNBC. https://www.cnbc.com/2022/04/16/these-skills-sepa rate-successful-kids-from-those-who-struggle-says-psychologist-parenting-expert.html

Boring, M. (2022, April 14). *Improve self-esteem, focus, and coordination with karate.* ADDitude. https://www.additudemag.com/kids-karate-adhd-focus-exercise/

Brain Art. (2022, March 21). *How art helps developing fine motor skills in children.* Brain Art. https://brainart.co/how-art-helps-developing-fine-motor-skills-in-children/#:~:

British Gymnastics. (2021, May 7). *Five benefits of taking part in recreational gymnastics.* British Gymnastics. https://www.british-gymnas tics.org/articles/five-benefits-for-your-child-taking-part-in-recreational-gymnastics

Buzanko, C. (2023, December 5). *ADHD emotional regulation for lids: An expert's guide for parents.* ADDitude. https://www.additudemag.com/ emotional-regulation-adhd-kids-strategies/#:~

Campo, N. (2022, September 7). *Why cycling might keep your kid's mental health in high gear.* National Geographic. https://www.nationalgeo graphic.co.uk/family/2022/09/why-cycling-might-keep-your-kids-mental-health-in-high-gear

CDC. (2021, January 26). *What is ADHD?* Centers for Disease Control and Prevention. https://www.cdc.gov/ncbddd/adhd/facts.html#:~

CDC. (2022, August 9). *Symptoms and diagnosis of ADHD.* Centers for Disease Control and Prevention. https://www.cdc.gov/ncbddd/ adhd/diagnosis.html

CDC. (2022, August 9). *Data and statistics about ADHD.* Centers for Disease Control and Prevention. https://www.cdc.gov/ncbddd/ adhd/data.html

Chan, Y.-S., Jang, J.-T., & Ho, C.-S. (2021). Effects of physical exercise in children with attention-deficit/hyperactivity disorder. *Biomedical Journal, 45*(2). https://doi.org/10.1016/j.bj.2021.11.011

Cherney, K. (2022, July 7). *Does ADHD get worse with age? Your FAQs.*

Healthline. https://www.healthline.com/health/adhd/can-adhd-get-worse-as-you-age#:~

Cleveland Clinic. (2017). *Attention deficit disorder (ADHD).* Cleveland Clinic. https://my.clevelandclinic.org/health/diseases/4784-atten tion-deficithyperactivity-disorder-adhd

Cleveland Clinic. (2022). *Basal ganglia: What it is, function & anatomy.* Cleveland Clinic. https://my.clevelandclinic.org/health/body/ 23962 basal-ganglia

Clifton, T. (2021, August 18). *Is roller skating good exercise?* Healthline. https://www.healthline.com/health/fitness/is-roller-skating-good-exercise

Cohen, D. (2023, October 30). *Why kids need to spend time in nature.* Child Mind Institute. https://childmind.org/article/why-kids-need-to-spend-time-in-nature/

Connaughton, M., O'Hanlon, E., Silk, T. J., Paterson, J., O'Neill, A., Anderson, V., Whelan, R., & McGrath, J. (2023). The limbic system in children and adolescents with attention-deficit/hyperactivity disorder: A longitudinal structural MRI analysis. *Biological Psychiatry Global Open Science.* https://doi.org/10.1016/j.bpsgos.2023. 10.005

Cooks-Campbell, A. (2022, July 27). *Social skills examples: How socializing can take you to the top.* Betterup. https://www.betterup.com/ blog/social-skills-examples

CPD. (2022). *Importance of repetition in learning.* CPC. https://cpduk.co. uk/news/importance-of-repetition-in-learning

Crichton-Stuart, C. (2020, December 10). *The top 10 benefits of eating healthy.* Medical News Today. https://www.medicalnewstoday. com/articles/322268

Cronkleton, E. (2021, August 13). *ADHD brain vs. normal brain: Function, differences, and more.* Medical News Today. https://www. medicalnewstoday.com/articles/adhd-brain-vs-normal-brain

Dancing for Children. (2022, February 7). *The benefits of dancing for children.* Carolina Dance. https://carolinadance.com/about/news/bene fits-of-dancing-for-children

Department of Education. (2016). *United States department of education office for civil rights.* https://www2.ed.gov/about/offices/list/ocr/

docs/dcl-know-rights-201607-504.pdf

DeSoto, L. (2023, June 6). *Why are carbohydrates important?* Verywell Health. https://www.verywellhealth.com/why-are-carbohydrates-important-7574416#:~

Diachenko, I., Kalishchuk, S., Zhylin, M., Kyyko, A., & Volkova, Y. (2022). Color education: A study on methods of influence on memory. *Heliyon, 8*(11), e11607. https://doi.org/10.1016/j.heliyon.2022.e11607

Dolin, A. (2023, October 11). *7 secrets to studying better with ADHD.* ADDitude. https://www.additudemag.com/learn-more-in-less-time/

Drake. (2023). *Sugar Consumption & ADHD: Does sugar make ADHD worse? Drake Institute.* https://www.drakeinstitute.com/sugar-consumption-and-adhd#:~:

Drinks, T. (2019, August 5). *Weighted blankets and ADHD.* Understood. https://www.understood.org/en/articles/weighted-blankets-and-adhd#:~:

Duggal, N. (2021, September 1). *Dopamine and attention deficit hyperactivity disorder(ADHD).* Healthline. https://www.healthline.com/health/adhd/adhd-dopamine#:~

ECMHC. (n.d.). *Stress and the developing brain* ECMHC. https://www.ecmhc.org/tutorials/trauma/mod2_3.html

Editors, Add. (2022a, March 16). *10 behavior chart rewards to motivate your child.* ADDitude. https://www.additudemag.com/slideshows/reward-systems-for-kids-with-adhd-unlock-better-behavior/

Editors, Add. (2022b, March 31). *How nutrition harmonizes the ADHD brain* ADDitude. https://www.additudemag.com/nutrition-harmonizes-adhd-brain/

Educate, J. K. (2023, June 30). *10+ benefits of volunteering for children.* JK Educate. https://www.jkeducate.co.uk/jk-expert-tips/the-benefits-of-volunteering-for-children/

Eske, J. (2019, August 19). *Dopamine vs. serotonin: Similarities, differences, and relationship.* MedicalNewsToday. https://www.medicalnewstoday.com/articles/326090

Fairbank, R. (2023). *An ADHD diagnosis in adulthood comes with challenges and benefits.* Apa.org. https://www.apa.org/monitor/2023/03/adult-adhd-diagnosis

Felton, A. (2022, September 1). *Limbic system: What to know.* WebMD. https://www.webmd.com/brain/limbic-system-what-to-know#:~:

Fletcher, J. (2019, May 3). *Foods for stabilizing insulin and blood sugar levels.* Medical news today. https://www.medicalnewstoday.com/articles/323529

G, D. (2023, May 8). *8 benefits of rock climbing for kids.* Brooklyn Boulders. https://brooklynboulders.com/blogs/news/8-benefits-of-rock-climbing-for-kids

Gallo, A. (2023, September 7). *6 little things you can do every day to make your child more independent.* Parents. https://www.parents.com/kids/development/little-things-you-can-do-every-day-to-make-your-child-more-independent/

Goally. (2023, July 14).Deep pressure sensory | ADHD & autism. Goally Apps & Tablets for Kids. https://getgoally.com/blog/deep-pressure-sensory-adhd-autism/

Gold, J. (2023, May 2). *Water features add architectural flair, wellness benefits and real estate enhancements to a home.* Forbes. https://www.forbes.com/sites/jamiegold/2023/05/02/water-features-add-architectural-flair-wellness-benefits-and-real-estate-enhancements-to-a-home/

Gordon, S. (2023, April 3). *Mental health benefits of cleaning and decluttering.*Verywell Mind. https://www.verywellmind.com/how-mental-health-and-cleaning-are-connected-5097496#:~:

Greene, L. (2023, October 30). *4 small ways to build confidence in kids.* Child Mind Institute. https://childmind.org/article/4-small-ways-to-build-confidence-in-kids/

Grimm, O., Kranz, T. M., & Reif, A. (2020). Genetics of ADHD: What should the clinician know?*Current Psychiatry Reports, 22*(4). https://doi.org/10.1007/s11920-020-1141-x

H.E. Luccock Quote. (n.d.). *A-Z Quotes.* https://www.azquotes.com/quote/1033014

Harris, N. (2023, May 20). *11 benefits of yoga for kids.* Parents. https://www.parents.com/benefits-of-yoga-for-kids-7406600

Harrison, J. R., Evans, S. W., Baran, A., Khondker, F., Press, K., Noel, D.,

Wasserman, S., Belmonte, C., & Mohlmann, M. (2020). Comparison of accommodations and interventions for youth with ADHD: A randomized controlled trial. *Journal of School Psychology, 80*, 15–36. https://doi.org/10.1016/j.jsp.2020.05.001

Harvard. (2021, March 6). *Foods linked to better brainpower.* Harvard Health. https://www.health.harvard.edu/healthbeat/foods-linked-to-better-brainpower#:~

Health Direct. (2018, July 2). *Developing life skills through sports.* Healthdirect. https://www.healthdirect.gov.au/developing-life-skills-through-sports

Heerema, E. (2022, September 17). *9 types of mnemonics to improve your memory.* Verywell Health. https://www.verywellhealth.com/memory-tip-1-keyword-mnemonics-98466

Holmes, B. (2023, July 17). *Revision flashcards: The key to effective study.* School Planner. https://www.schoolplanner.co.uk/blog/how-to-use-revision-flashcards/#:~:

Hovde, M. (2022, July 27). *ADHD and screen time: What's the link?* Psych Central. https://psychcentral.com/adhd/screen-time-and-children-with-adhd#research

Inercia. (2023, January 13). *Health and fitness benefits of inline skating.* Inercia. https://www.inercia.com/blog/en/health-and-fitness-benefits-of-inline-skating/

Jackson, A. (2023, May 5). *Harvard-trained expert shares her No. 1 strategy for getting people to trust you: "That's what I would do."* CNBC. https://www.cnbc.com/2023/05/05/harvard-trained-expert-active-listening-helps-people-trust-you.html

Jacobson, R. (2023, November 6). *School success Kit for kids with ADHD.* Child Mind Institute. https://childmind.org/article/school-success-kit-for-kids-with-adhd/#:~:

Jennings, K.-A. (2023, December 15). *11 best foods to boost your brain and memory.* Healthline. https://www.healthline.com/nutrition/11-brain-foods

Johnson, S. (2019, June 18). *What is the link between ADHD and dopamine?* MedicalNewsToday. https://www.medicalnewstoday.com/articles/325499

Josel, L. (2022a, January 23). *Pomodoro technique for ADHD kids: How to structure homework.* ADDitude. https://www.additudemag.com/pomodoro-focus-breaks-teens-adhd/#:~

Josel, L. (2022b, April 12). *Q: My disorganized teen hates checklists and charts.* ADDitude. https://www.additudemag.com/color-coding-organization-skills-adhd-teen/

Kaczegowicz, C. (2023, February 1). *Visual aids: A vital tool for students with ADHD.* Medium. https://medium.com/@ckaczeducation/visual-aids-a-vital-tool-for-students-with-adhd-bbf3a9eb5b25#:~:

Kessler, E. (2023). *IDEA and the IEP process.* Smart Kids. https://www.smartkidswithld.org/getting-help/know-your-childs-rights/idea-iep-process/

Klemm, P. (2023, February 25). *5 psychological benefits of horse riding for kids.* The Plaid Horse Magazine. https://www.theplaidhorse.com/2023/02/25/5-psychological-benefits-of-horse-riding-for-kids/#:~:

Kneisler, D. (2023, October 9). *World mental health day.* East Basildon Primary Care Network. https://www.eastbasildonpcn.nhs.uk/news/world-mental-health-day/#:~

Koseva, N. (2023a, July 3). *ADHD and anxiety in children: Understanding the connection and strategies for support.* The ADHD Centre. https://www.adhdcentre.co.uk/adhd-and-anxiety-in-children/

Koseva, N. (2023b, July 13). *Exploring the links between ADHD and environmental factors.* The ADHD Centre. https://www.adhdcentre.co.uk/exploring-the-links-between-adhd-and-environmental-factors/

Lahoti, A. (2023, February 28). *Dopamine and serotonin: Our own happy chemicals.* Nationwide Children's. https://www.nationwidechildrens.org/family-resources-education/700childrens/2023/02/dopamine-and-serotonin#:~:

Lastiri, L. (2023, August 25).How do you memorize things with ADHD? Iris Reading. https://irisreading.com/how-do-you-memorize-things-with-adhd/

Laurita, J. (2023, June 19). *The path to discipline: How martial arts instills and enhances discipline in adults.* The Desert Dojo. https://thedesertdojo.com/blog/the-path-to-discipline-how-martial-arts-instills-and-enhances-discipline-in-adults

Leahy, M. (2021, July 27). *Children with ADHD need positive reinforcement*

(*& other interventions that work*). ADDitude. https://www.addi
tudemag.com/adhd-in-children-signs-challenges-positive-
reinforcement/

Loeuy, K. J. (2022, April 11). Art for self-care and mental health.
University of Washington. https://thewholeu.uw.edu/2022/04/11/
art-for-self-care-and-mental-health/

Low, K. (2022, September 1). *How do section 504 accommodations help
students with ADHD?* Verywell Mind. https://www.verywellmind.
com/section-504-accommodations-students-adhd-20812

Low, K. (2019, October 28).Making your home more adhd-friendly for
your child. Verywell Mind. https://www.verywellmind.com/adhd-
friendly-ways-to-organize-a-home-20722#:~:

Lucchetti, L. (2023, October 13). *Benefits of outdoor play for children.*
Medical News Today. https://www.medicalnewstoday.com/arti
cles/outdoor-play-children

Mae, A. (2021, September 20). *ADHD sensory overload: Causes, treatment,
and more.* MedicalNewsToday. https://www.medicalnewstoday.
com/articles/adhd-sensory-overload

Main, P. (2021). *Working memory in the classroom.* Structural Learning.
https://www.structural-leearning.com/post/working-memory-in-
the-classroom-2

Mandriota, M. (2022, April 12). *ADHD and social skills: What to know.*
Psych Central. https://psychcentral.com/adhd/adhd-social-
skills#different-ages

Marner. (2023, October 23). *ADHD and artificial sweeteners.* ADDitude.
https://www.additudemag.com/adhd-and-artificial-sweeteners/

Mascott, A. (2022, June 7). *Why poetry matters.* Scholastic.https://www.
scholastic.com/parents/books-and-reading/raise-a-reader-blog/
why-poetry-matters.html

Massimine, C. (2023, January 26). *What's the future of coding?* Geek
Culture. https://medium.com/geekculture/whats-the-future-of-
coding-289dcda98327#:~:

Maynard, S. (2021, July 14). *Too much information.* ADDitude. https://
www.additudemag.com/too-much-information/

McLeod, S. (2018). *B.F. Skinner | Operant Conditioning.* Simply Psychology. https://www.simplypsychology.org/operant-conditioning. html#:~:

McQueen, J. (2022a, May 27). *Family therapy for childhood ADHD: What to know*. WebMD. https://www.webmd.com/add-adhd/childhood-adhd/childhood-adhd-family-therapy

McQueen, J. (2022b, May 28). *Childhood ADHD and screen time*. WebMD. https://www.webmd.com/add-adhd/childhood-adhd/childhood-adhd-screen-time

Mead, S. (2019). *6 self-esteem activities to help your child develop confidence*. Whitby. https://www.whitbyschool.org/passionforlearning/6-self-esteem-activities-to-help-your-child-develop-confidence

Mehren, A., Reichert, M., Coghill, D., Müller, H. H. O., Braun, N., & Philipsen, A. (2020). Physical exercise in attention deficit hyperactivity disorder – evidence and implications for the treatment of borderline personality disorder. *Borderline Personality Disorder and Emotion Dysregulation*, *7*(1). https://doi.org/10.1186/s40479-019-0115-2

Mind. (2021, November). *How nature benefits mental health*. Mind.https://www.mind.org.uk/information-support/tips-for-everyday-living/nature-and-mental-health/how-nature-benefits-mental-health/

Mind Mapping. (2023). *Mind mapping and ADHD*. SimpleMind. https://simplemind.eu/support/tutorials/mind-mapping-and-adhd/#:~:

Muppalla, S. K., Vuppalapati, S., Pulliahgaru, A. R., & Sreenivasulu, H. (2023). Effects of excessive screen time on child development: An updated review and strategies for management. *Cureus*, *15*(6). https://doi.org/10.7759/cureus.40608

MyBrainDr. (2023). *ADHD/ADD*. MyBrainDR. https://mybraindr.com/adhd-and-add-neurofeedback/#:~:

Neuropsychology, M., N. (2020, August 12). *ADHD superpowers*. Minnesota Neuropsychology, LLC. https://www.mnneuropsychology.com/articles/ADHD_Superpowers.html

NHS. (2017, October 18). *Food colours and hyperactivity*. Nhs.uk. https://www.nhs.uk/conditions/food-colours-and-hyperactivity/#:~

NHS. (2018a, June 1). *Attention deficit hyperactivity disorder (ADHD)* -

Causes. NHS. https://www.nhs.uk/conditions/attention-deficit-hyperactivity-disorder-adhd/causes/#:~

NHS. (2018b, June 1). *Attention deficit hyperactivity disorder (ADHD) - Living with.* NHS. https://www.nhs.uk/conditions/attention-deficit-hyperactivity-disorder-adhd/living-with/#:~:

NHS. (2018c, June 1). *Attention deficit hyperactivity disorder (ADHD) - Treatment.* NHS. https://www.nhs.uk/conditions/attention-deficit-hyperactivity-disorder-adhd/treatment/#:~:

NIMH. (2023). *Attention-Deficit/Hyperactivity Disorder.* National Institute of Mental Health (NIMH). https://www.nimh.nih.gov/health/topics/attention-deficit-hyperactivity-disorder-adhd#:~

Nurseline. (2023, November 21). *Food to avoid for ADHD individuals.* Nurselinecs. https://nurselinecs.co.uk/blog/food-to-avoid-for-adhd-individuals/#:~:

Nurture. (2023, May 22). *The benefits of gardening for children's wellbeing.* NurtureUK. https://www.nurtureuk.org/the-benefits-of-garden ing-for-childrens-wellbeing/

O'Donnell, L. (2018, June). *Disciplining your child (for parents).* Kids-Health. https://kidshealth.org/en/parents/discipline.html#:~:

O'Shea, C. (2016). *Individualized education programs (IEPs) (for parents) -* KidsHealth. https://kidshealth.org/en/parents/iep.html

Oliva, F., Malandrone, F., di Girolamo, G., Mirabella, S., Colombi, N., Carletto, S., & Ostacoli, L. (2021). The efficacy of mindfulness-based interventions in attention-deficit/hyperactivity disorder beyond core symptoms: A systematic review, meta-analysis, and meta-regression. *Journal of Affective Disorders, 292,* 475–486. https://doi.org/10.1016/j.jad.2021.05.068

Orlick, J. (2020, December 16). *Why structure and consistency are important for kids.* Kids Creek Therapy. https://www.kidscreektherapy.com/why-structure-and-consistency-are-important-for-kids/#:~:

Padayichie, K. (2023, June 15). *Collaborative learning.* Structural Learning. https://www.structural-learning.com/post/collaborative-learning

Patel, K. (2023, August 8). *How diet can help ADHD.* Dietitian Fit. https://dietitianfit.co.uk/how-diet-can-help-adhd/

Pebble. (2022, July 19). *7 benefits of drama classes for kids (and how to find the best one!)*. Pebble. https://bookpebble.co.uk/blog/7-reasons-why-drama-classes-are-good-for-kids-and-how-to-find-the-best-one

Pedersen, T. (2022, March 31). *Memory and mnemonic devices*. Psych Central. https://psychcentral.com/lib/memory-and-mnemonic-devices

Psychology Today. (2023). *Parenting a child with ADHD*. Psychology Today. https://www.psychologytoday.com/gb/basics/adhd/parenting-adhd-child#:~:

Pugle, M. (2021, December 16). *The ADHD brain vs. the non-ADHD brain*. Verywell Health. https://www.verywellhealth.com/adhd-brain-vs-normal-brain-5210534

Raising Children. (2017, June 5). *Nonverbal communication: Body language and tone of voice*. Raising Children Network. https://raisingchildren.net.au/toddlers/connecting-communicating/communicating/nonverbal-communication

Raza, D. (2022, May 16). *Why do People with ADHD find it hard to look into people's eyes?* ADHD Coaching. https://adhdcoachingaustralia.com.au/why-do-people-with-adhd-find-it-hard-to-look-into-peoples-eyes/

Roberts, M., Tolar-Peterson, T., Reynolds, A., Wall, C., Reeder, N., & Rico Mendez, G. (2022). The effects of nutritional interventions on the cognitive development of preschool-age children: A systematic review. *Nutrients, 14*(3), 532. https://doi.org/10.3390/nu14030532

Roggli, L. (2023, March 20). ADHD at the center: A whole-life, whole-person condition. *ADDitude*. https://www.additudemag.com/areas-of-life-health-relationships-career-adhd/

Roybal, B., Krueger, A., & Gopal, A. (2023, December 15). *ADHD diet and nutrition*. WebMD. https://www.webmd.com/add-adhd/adhd-diets

Russell, D. L. (2023, July 9). *ADHD sleep routine: A better bedtime for your child. They are the future*. https://www.theyarethefuture.co.uk/adhd-sleep-routine/#:~:

Sacks, J. (2017, June 6). *Play therapy interventions for ADHD: How does it work?* Tribeca Play Therapy. https://www.tribecaplaytherapy.com/

blog/2016/5/9/play-therapy-interventions-for-adhd-how-does-it-work

Santiago, D. (2020, March 23). *Four-box method and self-storage: Making decluttering easy* EasyStorage. https://www.easystorage.com/blog/four-box-method-and-self-storage-making-decluttering-easy#:~

Scandiffio, S. (2023, June 30). *9 important benefits of team sports for kids.* Active for Life. https://activeforlife.com/benefits-of-team-sports-for-kids/

Schewitz, K. (2023, October 19). *The olive oil on your salad isn't just tasty, it helps you to absorb vitamins. A dietitian shares 5 other healthy food pairings to try.* Insider. https://www.insider.com/how-to-increase-improve-nutrient-absorption-with-food-2023-10#:~:

Schrader, J. (2023, July 24). *Practicing the 5 C's of ADHD parenting.* Psychology Today. https://www.psychologytoday.com/gb/blog/promoting-empathy-with-your-teen/202307/practicing-the-5-cs-of-adhd-parenting#:~

Schultz, J. (2023, October 12). *Stressors and the aADHD brain pandemic coping advice.* ADDitude. https://www.additudemag.com/stressors-adhd-brain/

Seay, B., McCarthy, L., & Williams, P. (2019, September 13). *ADHD diagnosis and testing guide: Add symptom evaluations.* ADDitude. https://www.additudemag.com/adhd-testing-diagnosis-guide/

Segal, J., Smith, M., Robinson, L., & Boose, G. (2023, March 1). *Nonverbal communication and body language.* HelpGuide. https://www.helpguide.org/articles/relationships-communication/nonverbal-communication.htm

Seminara, D. (2023, February 19). *Why track and field is such a great kids' sport.* The Spectator World. https://thespectator.com/life/track-field-great-kids-sport/

Sensory. (2023). *Sensory overload in ADHD. Insights of a neurodivergent clinician.* Neurodivergent insights. https://neurodivergentinsights.com/blog/sensory-overload-in-adhd#:~:text=1.

Services, D. of H. & H. (2014, August 21). *Discipline and children.* Better-Health. https://www.betterhealth.vic.gov.au/health/healthyliving/discipline-and-children#:~

Sherman, C. (2023, October 23). Is ADHD a legal disability? Workplace legal protections for add. ADDitude. https://www.additudemag. com/workplace-legal-protection/#:~:text=Yes.

Sherman, C., Ramsay, J. R., & Barrow, K. (2017, January 27). *The truth about treating ADHD with cognitive behavioral therapy (CBT)*. ADDitude. https://www.additudemag.com/cognitive-behavioral-therapy-for-adhd/

Siggie, D. (2023, July 17). *17 quotes on being the calm in our kids' storm.* Youth Dynamics. https://www.youthdynamics.org/17-quotes-on-being-the-calm-in-our-kids-storm/

Sinfield, J. (2022, November 14). *How the ADHD brain biologically differs from the non-ADHD brain.* Verywell Mind. https://www.verywell mind.com/the-adhd-brain-4129396#:~:

Slade, B. (2023, November 16). *Small wins, big results: How to boost your child's confidence.* Medium. https://medium.com/@bslade/small-wins-big-results-how-to-boost-your-childs-confidence-9f3d0256eef8#:~:

Smith, K. (2023, February 13). *ADHD and screen time: How to steer kids away from too much technology.* Psycom. https://www.psycom.net/children-adhd-screen-fixation

Strauss, E. (2020, April 8). *The power of family dance parties when the world is falling apart.* CNN. https://edition.cnn.com/2020/04/08/health/family-dance-parties-coronavirus-wellness/index.html

Sutton, J. (2020, July 15). *What is mindful walking meditation and how can it impact your life?* PositivePsychology. https://positivepsychology.com/mindful-walking/

Tao, D., Gao, Y., Cole, A., Baker, J. S., Gu, Y., Supriya, R., Tong, T. K., Hu, Q., & Awan-Scully, R. (2022). The physiological and psychological benefits of dance and its effects on children and adolescents: A systematic review. *Frontiers in Physiology, 13*(925958). https://doi.org/10.3389/fphys.2022.925958

Tehrani-Doost, M., Noorazar, G., Shahrivar, Z., Banaraki, A. K., Beigi, P. F., & Noorian, N. (2017). Is emotion recognition related to core symptoms of childhood ADHD? *Journal of the Canadian Academy of Child and Adolescent Psychiatry = Journal de l'Academie Canadienne de Psychiatrie de l'Enfant et de L'adolescent, 26*(1), 31–38. https://www.ncbi.nlm.nih.gov/pmc/articles/PMC5349280/#:~:

TestPrepTraining. (2019, October 16). *Why you should take practice tests before an exam.* TestPrepTraining. https://www.testpreptraining. com/blog/why-you-should-take-practice-test/#:~:

Thriving with ADHD. (2018, June 30). *My number one ADHD parenting strategy.* Thriving with ADHD. https://thrivingwithadhd.com.au/ blog/my-number-one-adhd-parenting-strategy-listening-with-empathy/

Tori. (2020, April 10). *The power of photography on our kids' self-esteem.* Tori Deslauriers. https://torideslauriers.com/power-of-photogra phy-on-our-kids-self-esteem/

Turis, S. (2021, June 2). *Yoga for kids with ADHD: Sports and activities.* ADDitude. https://www.additudemag.com/yoga-for-kids-with-adhd/#:~:

Turk, A., Lotfi Marchoubeh, M., Fritsch, I., Maguire, G. A., & Sheikh-Bahaei, S. (2021). Dopamine, vocalization, and astrocytes. *Brain and Language, 219,* 104970. https://doi.org/10.1016/j.bandl.2021. 104970

Tutorful. (2023, February 17). *Tutorful - 6 amazing benefits of music lessons for children.* Tutorful. https://tutorful.co.uk/blog/6-amazing-benefits-of-music-lessons-for-children

Van De Hey, E. (2023, January 28). *The power of positive reinforcement.* LinkedIn. https://www.linkedin.com/pulse/power-positive-rein forcement-ethan-van-de-hey

Vanbuskirk, S. (2022, April 8). *When ADHD is all in the family.* ADDi-tude. https://www.additudemag.com/is-adhd-hereditary-blog/

Vierstra, G. (2023). *ADHD teaching strategies.* Understood. https://www. understood.org/en/articles/adhd-teaching-strategies

Villagomez, A., & Ramtekkar, U. (2014). Iron, magnesium, vitamin D, and zinc deficiencies in children presenting with symptoms of attention-deficit/Hyperactivity disorder. *Children, 1*(3), 261–279. https://doi.org/10.3390/children1030261

Weinstein, T. (2022, December 22). *How brown noise for ADHD can help teens focus and relax.* Newport Academy. https://www.newportacad emy.com/resources/empowering-teens/brown-noise-for-adhd/#:~:

Wellness Centre. (2019, October 23). *10 incredible benefits of playing with lego®*. Children's Wellness Centre. https://www.childrenswellness centre.co.uk/10-incredible-benefits-of-playing-with-lego-2/

WGU. (2021, August 11). *Harnessing parent-teacher collaboration.* Western Governors University. https://www.wgu.edu/blog/ harnessing-parent-teacher-collaboration2107.html#:~:

Whiteford, A. (2019, January 17). *The benefits of cooking with kids.* Healthy Little Foodies. https://www.healthylittlefoodies.com/the-benefits-of-cooking-with-kids/

Wilkins, F. (2023, October 23). *How is the ADHD brain different?* Child Mind Institute. https://childmind.org/article/how-is-the-adhd-brain-different/#:~

Williamson, T. (2021, June 21). *20 self-esteem activities for kids guaranteed to build confidence.* Mindfulmazing. https://www.mindfulmazing. com/20-self-esteem-activities-for-kids/

Willis, A. (2023, January 17). *Why your child should learn to swim.* Virgin Active. https://www.virginactive.co.uk/blogs/articles/2023/01/17/ benefits-of-kids-swim

Printed in Great Britain
by Amazon

43979285R00109